THE ART OF HOSPITALITY

YVONNE G. BAKER

ACCENT BOOKS
Denver, Colorado

ACCENT BOOKS

A division of Accent Publications, Inc.
12100 West Sixth Avenue
P.O. Box 15337
Denver, Colorado 80215

Library of Congress Catalog Card Number 86-70117

ISBN 0-89636-208-6

Cover design by J. William Coburn

CONTENTS

Acknowledgments

Some of the recipes in this book previously appeared in
Today's Christian Woman.

All Scripture quoted is from the New International Version.

Dedication

TO THE BURTON FAMILY
—whose lives personify gracious
and caring hospitality

And over all these virtues put on love, which binds them all together in perfect unity.

Colossians 3:14

IN THE BEGINNING

I was terrified.

There sat two huge frozen turkeys. Bags full of groceries. A big church kitchen filled with unfamiliar utensils. And tomorrow I was supposed to have a Thanksgiving dinner prepared for twenty-five people.

It had seemed like such a good idea when I volunteered for the job—to make a meal for people who would be lonely over that holiday. It was a way for our small youth group to share a bit of the caring and concern that our Lord had given to us. But right now those great ideas had faded from my mind. I was sixteen years old, and I didn't know where to start.

Somehow, though, I got through the dinner, and nobody got food poisoning or complained because the mashed potatoes were a bit runny.

That was over twenty years ago.

It's been twenty years filled with the preparation of hundreds of meals for youth groups, church groups and individual families. Years where I owned my own cooking school and catering business, where I wrote a newspaper column on food, and authored six cookbooks. Years of failures and frustrations and tiredness mixed with the joy of seeing loneliness flee and hearts lifted while sharing food and time.

All of these experiences form the basis for this book. It is the fruit of many years, of trial and error, of happiness and satisfaction, and of all the intangible ingredients that make up the art of hospitality. This book is my gift to you with the prayer that the Lord will use it in your life to minister His love to His needy world.

CHARACTERISTICS OF A HOSTESS

You can be a successful, creative, hostess!

How do I know you can? Because Romans 12:13 says, "practice hospitality." God never gives us a command that is impossible for us to fulfill nor are any given to cause us guilt and frustration. What He commands, He gives the grace to do, and in doing His commands, we find joy and satisfaction.

We can assume, then, that hospitality is very important to God. It is a reflection of His gracious character. He welcomes and loves us in spite of our sins and shortcomings. Thus, when we exercise hospitality, it can be a way of saying "thank you" to God as well as a way of sharing His love with others.

Hospitality is mentioned numerous other times in the New Testament. Let's consider these passages:

"Now the overseer must be above reproach, the husband of but one wife, temperate, self-controlled, respectable, hospitable, able to teach." I Timothy 3:2

In speaking about the godly widow, the Bible says she must be *". . . well-known for her good deeds, such as bringing up children, showing hospitality, washing the feet of the saints, helping those in trouble and devoting herself to all kinds of good deeds."* I Timothy 5:10

9

Hebrews 13:1-2 say, *"Keep on loving each other as brothers. Do not forget to entertain strangers, for by so doing some people have entertained angels without knowing it."*

And I Peter 4:9 commands, *"Offer hospitality to one another without grumbling."*

I especially like that passage in Peter—reminding us not to grumble when we practice hospitality. It isn't easy to be a gracious hostess today, and I imagine it wasn't any easier in Peter's time. He probably would not have included the command to practice hospitality without grumbling if there had not been quite a bit of it going on even back then. I can just imagine the talk as Paul's next visit to Jerusalem neared, "Who wants to entertain that eccentric missionary? And as if he isn't bad enough, he's always bringing *Gentiles* along. No proper Jew should have these people in their home let alone *eat* with them. And Paul never even appreciates the trouble he causes; he just preaches at people for their bad attitude . . . . " And on and on and on. So Peter commanded them just to do it and not complain.

I think one reason hospitality is so scary is that we see it as a difficult skill—entertaining people, preparing meals, planning banquets. There *are* some difficult things about it, but like any other skill, it is one that can be mastered with a bit of trial and error, a few frustrations and lots of successes. Most importantly, when we realize hospitality is just another skill, we can develop a plan to learn it. Nobody is born with the ability to ski perfectly, and no one is born with a perfect dinner-party-producing gene. All of our skills in life are developed bit by bit—and sometimes by falling on one's face in the process.

Once we realize that hospitality is a skill to be learned, it can relieve the guilt of someone who has reached adulthood and does not know how to cook or to entertain. I met numerous women in my cooking classes who felt as though something was wrong with them because they couldn't put on a dinner party for eight. In talking with them, I found that many of them had mothers who had worked—a great contrast from the farm days when Sunday dinner was an event a girl helped prepare from the time she was old enough to peel potatoes. Many women don't know how to entertain because they didn't learn how as they were growing up. And there is absolutely nothing wrong with you, your family or your childhood if that is your situation. You simply have the joy of learning this delightful new area of skills as an adult.

This book will give you step-by-step help as you develop your hospitality skills. But first, let's begin by considering the characteristics of a successful Christian hostess. And if you feel you don't possess all of them at the present time, let them become goals to keep in mind mentally and in prayer. You don't become a good skier by just watching the beginners, you must try to imitate the professional instructor. This list is a bit like that—a description of the hostess we all want to become.

It is important to remember, too, that the list is descriptive of a *Christian* hostess. The primary focus of Christian hospitality is not to keep up with the latest trends, to impress people or to advance ourselves. The primary focus of Christian hospitality is to love each other in a tangible, touchable, sharing way.

With these thoughts in mind, let's look at the characteristics of a Christian hostess.

She Has the Right Attitude

> *Finally, brothers, whatever is true, whatever is noble, whatever is right, whatever is pure, whatever is lovely, whatever is admirable—if anything is excellent or praiseworthy—think about such things.*
>
> Philippians 4:8

We always have a choice in our attitudes. And this is especially true in the area of hospitality. We can either think about the mound of dishes we will have to wash up or the people we are encouraging. We can think about the destruction of our tidy house, or that our kids can share a home with their friends.

The importance of a right attitude was made real to me one day when I was inwardly complaining about how much cooking I had to do. Nobody ever seemed to invite my family to dinner; I was always expected to cook the holiday meals, fix the Sunday meals, give the baby showers, etc. I felt quite the martyr.

In the midst of this great pity party, it was almost as if I could hear the Lord say to me, "But child, you have food. Not only do you have food, but you have food enough to share and the strength to cook it."

I felt so ashamed.

This was during the time when the first news of the famine in Ethiopia was broadcast. I realized then that attitude is what makes the difference between hospitality being drudgery or joyful service.

It's important to form the habit of mentally listing the positive aspects of your hospitality:

● We get to show the new family at church that we care for strangers.

● Our children get to see that even if Sandra is pregnant and not married, that a family cares enough to see she has friends and a healthy baby.

● Our son knows he can always bring the baseball team to our house for great snacks so they won't loiter around the field.

● The family that just immigrated from Korea will get to know the people in the church and feel loved as we take turns having them over one night each week.

● Karen's kids can come and play with my kids and husband after dinner on Sunday. She and I can talk and her sons will have a male role model in their lives after their dad's death.

The list could go on and on, but when you think about it, the seemingly "little" moments of hospitality, a dinner or an afternoon or a home shared, can be literally life-changing events. When you "think on these things," your hands will fly through the work and your heart will be in it.

She Is Organized

Being organized means being in control. When you are in control of the details of entertaining, it becomes a joy you participate in instead of a nightmare you live through. Though this book will give you numerous ideas on organization, one of the most important and useful organizational tools is a hospitality planning notebook. It will be your portable planning, inspiration and organization center. As you go through this book you can copy ideas into certain sections or list page numbers for reference. Here is how to set one up:

(1) Make yourself a hospitality planning notebook from a

large looseleaf notebook with several dividers. The sections will be discussed below. Also purchase some of the inserts for notebooks that have pockets so you can put in useful clippings from newspapers and magazines.

(2) The first section can be *Inspirations for Hospitality*. In this you can write out the characteristics of hostesses you admire, or little things they have done that made you feel welcome. You can also include Scripture verses, stories and examples that encourage you to practice hospitality.

(3) One section of the notebook should be your *Master Planning* section. Before planning any event, take time to sit down with pencil and paper and write out every aspect of the party or meal. Include the purpose of the event, the guest list, the menu, any activities you want to include, and decorations or special supplies you will need.

Once you get the overall plan written down, write out a timetable for accomplishing each task. Place the date to complete that task on your calendar or have a checklist in your notebook. Other sections in this book will give you more details on how to do this. It is much easier to have everything written down where you can refer to it while planning a party or dinner than to try carrying every idea in your head.

(4) Another, *Previous Parties*, section can keep track of your hospitality events of the past. In this section list who came for dinners or parties or as houseguests. Write down the menu(s) served and the response to it. Write down any special likes or dislikes of your guests in this section. With this handy reference, you won't get into the habit of inviting the same people or serving the same menu again and again. And, you'll remember that when a favorite aunt stays with you, she loves orange juice but is allergic to apple juice.

In this section you can also write down future ideas. For example, perhaps when you invited Jane and Jeff over for dinner, Jane mentioned that she just loved carrot cake. Make a little note to yourself that next time you have them over you'd like to make carrot cake. Your thoughtfulness in remembering these sorts of details about people's preferences will always be appreciated.

(5) One section can be devoted to *Food Menu Ideas*. The section on specific parties will contain some menus, but here you can add others of your own. Write out menu combinations that have worked well in the past. Beside each menu item place the cookbook and page number where they can be found. Also record party menus and variations that worked well. This can save a tremendous amount of planning time and you won't have to start from scratch each time you set out to plan a party. To get you started, there are sample menus in chapter eight. If you want to be super organized, you can number each menu plan, and then simply put the number beside your record of what guests you have entertained at various times.

(6) Another division is an *Idea* section. When you see a picture in a magazine of a table setting or food presentation you find especially lovely, cut it out and place it in your notebook. You might want to subdivide this section between food serving, garnishing ideas, and decorating ideas. You could also have a game and activity section if you desire. See chapter five for ideas on this.

(7) The final section should be *Resources*. Since there will be times when you are unable to handle every bit of entertaining yourself, this section can record the name, phone number and some cost estimates of caterers and other specialty food stores that will make up party platters. You can also record rental information and cost sheets. Names of teenagers who are able to help serve and clean up for a party, and any other pertinant people such as clowns who can be

hired for children's parties should also be included in this section.

She Is Creative

When the world was created, the Bible tells us it was made from nothing by God. Sometimes, when we practice hospitality, we must act in His image and also create beauty out of seemingly nothing. We may have very little money or time or talent, but we still want to share our hearts and homes with those we love. Creativity enables us to accomplish this.

Creativity makes decorations out of cast-off toys and dried, roadside flowers.

Creativity makes scrambled eggs a feast served by candle-light.

Creativity gathers together single friends who each bring one pizza ingredient and share the work and clean-up.

Creativity is having your children tell you the kind of party *they* want, and—within reason—trying to make it real.

Creativity is often just asking the Lord for new eyes to see situations differently: to look at what you have and to think about what you can do with it instead of feeling frustrated and wishing you had more.

She Has a Sense of Humor

Humor is an essential ingredient in hospitality.

I'll never forget the time I was entertaining some friends from out of town. It was important to me to make a nice meal. But just as I was folding the whipped cream into the fruit salad, I became distracted about something and the whole thing landed on the floor.

I almost cried—whipped cream and fancy fruits were not part of my regular food budget. At that same instant, I remembered I'd carefully cleaned the kitchen floor earlier and so I carefully scooped up the salad and replaced it in the bowl. By this time I was laughing at myself and, in all honesty, had to tell my guests why. Instead of my being upset and making people feel awkward, we all had a good laugh.

Humor can turn tears into laughter in many similar situations. I tend to burn muffins and biscuits. Laughter makes me cut the bottoms off and tell my guests that makes them easier to butter.

Whenever anything awkward happens, laugh at it and have your guests laugh with you. What seems a tragedy today, if handled with a light touch, will often provide treasured memories among friends for years to come.

She Is Flexible

This characteristic goes along with a sense of humor. It means not taking too seriously any aspect of entertaining. If you remain flexible through every aspect of entertaining, you and your guests will have a much better time. Below are some examples of flexibility at different stages in the entertainment process.

(1) In planning any event, have a variety of dates and people to invite. Everyone has such extremely complex schedules and lifestyles now that you have to adjust to them. For instance, a few years ago, I wanted two pastor friends of mine to meet each other. Because both had extremely busy

schedules, we literally had to plan three months ahead for a time when both of them would be in town. Of course I wanted to have people over for dinner during the three months, so I had to do a bit of juggling with various schedules in order to have other combinations of people over before I could work out the dinner party with my pastor friends.

Accepting the busy schedules of other people, and being flexible in light of them, is a kind and a gracious way to treat others. People often feel overextended and overscheduled. But if a friend is understanding and willing to take the time to schedule a get-together—even if it means planning a few months ahead—you can be sure it will be greatly appreciated.

(2) In planning your menu, always check with your guests to find out diet limitations. Many people have restricted diets, some out of convictions, some out of medical necessity. In my closest circle of friends I have found the following limitations: one individual who does not eat any sugar; one couple who will not eat any red meat; a male friend who is a complete vegetarian; another couple who must severely restrict saturated fat intake; one woman who cannot eat wheat or dairy products; one man who cannot tolerate even moderately spicy foods, and several others whose idea of dessert is chocolate only. In addition, you need to know even the simplest preferences—such as if your guests are coffee or tea drinkers or if they drink only decaffeinated products.

In your hospitality notebook, you can record these limitations and consult it when you plan your menus. Always ask new friends if they have any food limitations or preferences. Then when you plan your guest lists, it is much easier, for example, to invite all the vegetarians at the same time. If you can't do that, you might need to make some changes in your menu.

For instance, you want to make lasagna. Some people you want to invite are vegetarians, some enjoy natural foods and some don't care what they eat. To satisfy everyone, you can alter your lasagna recipe from the regular hamburger variety to a spinach lasagna with whole wheat noodles. (There is an excellent Spinach Lasagna recipe in the Main Dishes section that works great for just this sort of situation.)

Another hint on menu planning: Never make guests feel awkward because they have a dietary limitation. Simply serve the meal without commenting on the person for whom it may be tailored.

Remember, too, that ethnic cooking is often a way to have meals that satisfy everyone without making anyone feel awkward. A Chinese stir-fried main dish can be made in a healthful, vegetarian way to please any taste. Many Mexican and Italian dishes can be made in the same way.

(3) Be flexible in your table settings. If you don't have enough dishes or placemats of the same pattern, mix and match them. Some people set fascinating tables using a variety of patterns they have picked up at garage sales and secondhand stores. If you are serving a huge crowd, use paper or plastic ware. Many restaurant supply houses or discount outlets sell this sort of paper ware in large quantities at a substantial savings.

If you don't have room for a large sitdown dinner, have a buffet. If you don't have enough chairs, make the event very casual so your guests are comfortable sitting on the floor. If your place is too small for a buffet, plan a picnic.

There is no perfect way to entertain. Being flexible makes the setting fit the lifestyle and budget that is perfect for you.

(4) Be flexible at the event itself. If someone has to bring a child you didn't count on, if another cancels out, if someone is late because of an emergency, if an unexpected guest arrives with one of your guests, what do you do?

Relax. If you've been flexible in your planning, you may have some toys on hand for the child, an extra plate, silverware and a seating plan for the unexpected guest; and for someone who's late, your initial flexibility in menu planning has you serving items that can stay on warm in the oven without loss of quality or taste. (The recipe section is designed with things like this in mind.)

Think through possible problems ahead of time. Sort of in the same way a fire drill at school taught you what to do in an emergency situation, run through a little entertainment "fire" drill in your mind. Ask yourself what would you do if:

If Stephanie brings her children, do I have a few coloring books and some simple puzzles and toys they could play with while we have tea?

If there's a possibility John might bring his cousin, maybe I should make a large casserole instead of individual meat entrees.

If Ken and Patti are late because they have to drive so far, maybe I'll make a chicken dish that will taste good even if it has to wait on warm in the oven for half an hour.

Once you know what you would do in the event of an emergency, you won't be devastated when one happens.

She Puts Others First

Being a gracious hostess is often not easy or convenient.

We have our own projects, schedules and priorities. Especially with houseguests, very young or older guests, our lives can be interrupted.

Remembering Jesus' example in John 13 is helpful at these times. In the ancient world, the job of washing the guests' feet was done by a servant. After walking the dusty, dirty roads, I imagine those feet weren't very attractive or pleasant—obviously all the disciples thought so because, not having a servant, none of them volunteered for the job.

So Jesus did it. Their master, the one who was about to die for them (and us!), during his last meal with his friends did the dirty work. And often we, too, have reasons for not wanting to do the extra things for our guests. We are tired or busy or don't feel quite well—but Jesus was about to die and He willingly accepted the responsibilities of a host.

This is not meant to induce guilt. The Lord doesn't ask any of us to become martyrs from constant serving. The point here is that hospitality should be practiced for the sake of others, and it is less than honest if we do not admit that it is not always easy. Sometimes it is pure joy and we love it as much as our guests. But sometimes it requires a sheer act of the will to put our guests first and to remember Jesus' words:

"Now that I, your Lord and Teacher, have washed your feet, you also should wash one another's feet. I have set you an example that you should do as I have done for you. I tell you the truth, no servant is greater than his master, nor is a messenger greater than the one who sent him. Now that you know these things, you will be blessed if you do them."

John 13:14-17

She Is Loved By God

The Christian hostess has a unique perspective. As satisfying as a perfect dinner party for eight, a relaxed buffet for thirty with authentic ethnic food and decorations, or a memorable wedding brunch might be to give, the Christian hostess has another satisfaction.

For her the rewards of entertaining reach into eternity. Every struggle to make a recipe work, every hour spent making a special food for someone who needs to experience love, every penny saved so a guest could share a meal—our gracious Lord notes and remembers. Not only that, but when we practice hospitality, Jesus literally takes it quite personally. In Matthew 25:31-40, He tells us that when we have shared our food with the hungry—and I think that means not only those hungry for physical food, but also those hungry for love, fellowship and acceptance—it is just like doing it for Jesus Himself.

It is exciting to think about those verses. Ask God to help you remember that what you are doing, you are doing for Him. Ask Him to allow you to see the work as a gift, an offering of love to the Savior you serve. Ask Him to allow you to sense His smile of approval until the day you see Him face to face and hear Him say, "Come, you who are blessed by my Father; take your inheritance, the kingdom prepared for you since the creation of the world . . . . I tell you the truth, whatever you did for one of the least of these brothers of mine, you did for me" (Matthew 25:34,40).

Conclusion

The old saying that "practice makes perfect" is as true in

being a hostess as in any other area. Look over the characteristics listed above from time to time. Think about them. Pray about them. Practice them even one at a time. And before you know it, they will become a part of your life.

Because of the service by which you have proved yourselves, men will praise God for the obedience that accompanies your confession of the gospel of Christ, and for your generosity in sharing with them and with everyone else. And in their prayers for you their hearts will go out to you, because of the surpassing grace God has given you.

II Corinthians 9:13-14

THE QUESTION OF MANNERS

In everything, do to others what you would have them do to you, for this sums up the Law and the Prophets.

Matthew 7:12

The Golden Rule really says it all, doesn't it? The contents of every etiquette book in the world can be summed up by saying that one ought to treat others as we wish to be treated ourselves.

Why then all the concern and worry about the subject of manners? About what is proper and what is not? About what to do and how to dress and what to say in certain situations?

I think it is because we *do care* about others. I think we honestly wonder what is expected of us, and what will make other people happy and comfortable. We want to treat others with kindness and concern and in a proper manner. We want to do the right thing at the right time. But in spite of all these good intentions, sometimes we honestly don't know what the proper and kind manner is for a certain occasion.

There are a number of reasons for this. Our society is not

the homogeneous world it once was. People are constantly on the move, communities have few continuing traditions, families rarely pass down heirloom silver and china, life is far more spontaneous and casual than it was in the past. In addition, many of our personal histories leave us uncertain in the area of manners. Kathy knows that what may be all right for a casual dinner at home might not be proper for a formal church banquet. Margarete grew up in a home where not much entertaining went on and she feels uncomfortable because she's never learned what is expected of a hostess.

This is where a knowledge of manners is useful. Manners provide a set of guidelines which can help ease a situation in which you are uncertain, or where you have had little experience, or are simply confused. What might be proper in one setting or situation, may not be proper in another. What might be useful for a certain group of people, may not be for another. Manners answer questions and clear the way in these troublesome situations.

As important as these guidelines are, keep in mind that this section will not attempt to answer every possible question on the subject. If you are interested in more detail or find yourself in a very specialized situation, such as meeting the Queen of England or having an ambassador to dinner, there are numerous, excellent books available at any public library.

This chapter will attempt to outline some basic reminders and set forth some guidelines for Christians who want to make all their guests feel comfortable in any situation.

First, we'll discuss the expectations of hostess and guests. Then we'll cover different kinds of hospitality and give suggestions for them. Finally, there will be some suggestions concerning specifically Christian etiquette. This section will primarily cover manners for one time occasions such as dinners and other parties. Manners for extended visits and overnight guests will be dealt with in a later chapter on that subject.

Manners Of the Hostess

(1) The first responsibility of a hostess is a sort of balancing act. She must prepare as completely as possible but, at the same time, act as if it were absolutely no trouble at all. There are few worse situations than a hostess who either subtly or directly makes her guests aware of how much work was involved in her preparation.

Tangible ways to express this balance include:

● Prepare the food in advance. Everything that can be done ahead should be done ahead. Let it either warm in the oven or chill in the refrigerator. Have the appetizer(s) already set out. It is fine to leisurely toss the salad or garnish the main dish after your guests arrive, but the majority of work or elaborate preparations should be taken care of before guests arrive. The recipe section will give you numerous recipes to let you do this easily.

● Be sure the table is already set either for a sit-down dinner or for a buffet. A beautifully set table gives the impression that guests were eagerly anticipated.

● Clean the house early in the day or the evening before so that you aren't fluffing up pillows or picking up toys as the guests knock at the door. I have been known to gather up a huge pile of dirty dishes and hide them behind the shower curtain, but at least I wasn't frantically washing dishes as the guests arrived.

● Try to time your preparation activities so you are

finished at least ten minutes before your guests arrive. Then sit down, have a cup of tea, and ask the Lord's blessing on the time ahead. Ask that you have a sensitive heart to the needs of your guests; ask that the practical details go well; ask that you be a channel of God's love.

(2) Be sure to invite guests as far in advance as possible. Although last minute invitations are fun for close friends, for people with children, distances to travel, busy jobs or just the complications of modern life, being able to plan ahead is a much appreciated courtesy.

(3) The hostess should dress simply, attractively and appropriately for the occasion. It is not kind to tell guests it is a casual event and then dress in an elaborate hostess outfit. Also, be sure to wear something that is easy to move in and comfortable for serving food and taking care of last minute details. A full apron is useful. If you have long hair, and are involved in quite a bit of food preparation, try to wear it up.

(4) Let your guests know how much you appreciate them taking the time to be with you. Personally greet each guest as they arrive, express how happy you are to have them. When they leave, be sure to see them to the door.

(5) No matter what has gone wrong, or how inadequate you might feel about a certain aspect of your entertaining, never run yourself down or apologize for not having this or that. Though those kinds of statements are sometimes intended to express humility, they may make guests uncomfortable and leave them wondering what standard of perfection you expect when they entertain you. Also, avoid any comparisons between your guest's cooking and yours. While intended as a compliment, it can make your guest feel uncomfortable.

(6) A hostess has several responsibilities at the dinner table. First of all, place your fork on your plate as soon as

everyone is served, even if you don't take a quick mouthful, to signal that it is all right for your guests to begin eating. A hostess should never finish before the slowest eater, either, which may necessitate nibbling on food even if you are full. The hostess should also take at least a token second helping and encourage guests to do so. She is also a traffic controller at the table making sure the butter is passed along and noticing if someone is out of a certain item and appears rather shy about asking for it. At such times she can say, "Jane, could you pass me the salad, please," and add, "oh, Allen, why don't you help yourself on the way?"

(7) The hostess should make sure there are enough bathroom linens and soap. It is a nice touch to have paper cups in the bathroom as well as hair spray and hand lotion for the use of guests. It is also important to have a place for coats where they will not be crushed or crowded. Clean out a coat closet if possible, or if you are having a really large party, you can rent a coat rack for nominal cost.

(8) It is, of course, the responsibility of the host and hostess to make introductions. If the party is very large, like an open house or a large event at church, you may want to ask a few friends to also help introduce people to each other. One friend of mine, Cathey, is invaluable at parties in this way. She always seems to notice people who don't know other people. She goes over, introduces herself, and then introduces them to several others. It is a relaxing joy to know she is there.

(9) For formal situations, a brief review on introductions might be helpful: Introduce the least important person to the most important person. Introduce men to women, and younger people to older people.

(10) It is helpful to give total strangers more than a name in order to get a conversation started. For example, you

might say, "Mary, this is John Aimes. John, Mary is also a journalism major. She might like to hear about your internship with the newspaper." Or, "Mrs. Dunston, may I introduce Cheryl Tomas. Cheryl just became the director of the children's choir that I believe your daughter is entering."

Introductions can be useful in other ways, too, such as letting someone know that a certain person is new in town, is looking for a house or work or a school. People enjoy being helpful and letting them know a need exists is often all it takes to get a very useful exchange started.

Serious concerns aside, any item of similar interest between two people who have just met is good to include in the introduction. If you can't think of anything, mention something about the person, their job, a hobby, or any other tidbit that might be interesting.

(11) Be sure to spend time talking with each of your guests. Saying that a party is too large is no excuse. A frantic host or hostess relaxes no one. A few minutes of conversation makes everyone feel welcome.

(12) Finally, another important area of balance is to stay away from extremely impressive, extravagant entertaining even if you are able to do it and can afford it. You want to do special things for your guests—a nice dinner, a tidy house, pleasant guests, but don't feel you have to do extraordinary things. Your guests may feel they can never repay that sort of hospitality.

Etiquette For the Guest

(1) Be honest with yourself and your hostess when asked to a particular event. Say "no" if you are overextended, exhausted, or would be unable to be a good guest. It helps no

one if you accept invitations you will resent, or if you have a conflicting event and can only attend part of an evening at one event. Let your hostess know the reasons you cannot attend, assure her of your appreciation, and, if possible, suggest an alternative time to see her. For example, you might say, "Georgia, I'm so sorry Jim and I can't come to dinner on Saturday. We have been tied up with teacher training classes every night this week, but I would love to get together with you. Would you be free for coffee sometime early next week?" A reply like that lets her know that though you have rejected an invitation, you haven't rejected the person.

(2) Be sure you know what sort of an event you've been invited to and what to wear. A hostess never minds being asked what she is wearing and to wear a similar piece of clothing is always appropriate. If you don't have a chance to ask, or for some reason show up in an entirely incorrect outfit, you may quietly apologize to your hostess. Other than that, do not mention a word of what you are wearing to anyone else—if you are terribly underdressed people may think you are promoting some cause, if you are overdressed, you may be seen as charmingly eccentric.

(3) Of course you should be on time for any invitation or call if you will be more than about ten minutes late. At the same time, never arrive early. A guest who arrives while the hostess is frantically getting last minute things done will only cause her more stress.

(4) Hostess gifts are a gracious and thoughtful gesture. Flowers are always appreciated. A bouquet of fresh flowers from your garden, or even one rose, is as nice as an elaborate bouquet. All sorts of other little items are also nice. Dessert candies such as chocolates or exotic mints are wonderful. Fancy nuts, a wedge of unusual cheese, a special ice cream

topping, a homemade jam or any special food treat you know your hosts might enjoy. A special tea or coffee is also an appropriate gift. The cost is not important and should not be great, but it is nice to show your appreciation in a tangible way. If you keep a small supply of gifts on hand, such as small packets of special teas or little containers of jam, you will always have one ready to take with you.

(5) Do your part to contribute to the success of the gathering. If the hostess is especially busy and you did not get introduced to someone, introduce yourself. Initiate conversations, be kind to difficult people, try to make the people around you comfortable. It is guaranteed that people will think you are an excellent conversationalist if you ask them about themselves.

If you aren't in the habit of asking questions during a conversation, stop for a minute and ask yourself what do you really know about your friends? Do you know where they grew up and how they felt about their childhood? Do they have brothers or sisters? If so and they live far away, do they miss them? You might know what they do for a living, but do you know how they really feel about their job, or what they like or dislike about it most? Do you know what their dreams are? Do you know anything about how they came to know the Lord or where they are in their Christian life? Do you know what convictions they struggle with, what doubts they have? Taking time to find the answers to these and other questions can deepen and strengthen any relationship.

Think about the last time anyone asked you questions like that, listened to the answers, and didn't give advice or judgment. (Questions from a paid therapist don't count.) You know the lonely place in your heart that cries for concern like that from others—give your friends that gift.

(6) Be sure to take time to compliment your hostess and

host. Be especially sensitive to areas you know are difficult for them. For example, if your hostess is just learning to cook, be sure to compliment her on the food. If the bathroom is newly wallpapered, be sure to notice. Thank them for their time and effort; for caring enough to include you in their lives.

(7) Some guests feel they must help clean up. If you can do so in an unobtrusive way, removing plates, cups, and other items at a large party is always helpful, as is helping to clear dishes from the table. Beyond that you may offer to help, but if the hostess turns you down, do not press the issue. Many people do not want to clean up when guests are present, many have their own ways of doing things, and some prefer tackling those tasks alone.

(8) Following any event, thank-yous are never outdated. A phone call may be adequate for a very casual dinner party with close friends, but a brief written note is always appreciated. It takes only a few minutes to write but that minute of caring is important.

(9) Return invitations. Years ago this was not even a matter for discussion. If one accepted hospitality, it was expected it would be returned in one form or another. If a single gentleman was invited to dinner and did not have a place in which to reciprocate, he took guests to a restaurant. If one could not afford a fancy dinner, one offered tea. Today many people say they are too busy, have too much work, or too many responsibilities. Other excuses are, "I'm single and my place is too small." "I teach a class, pastor a church (or fill any other position of leadership) and I just can't entertain everyone, so I won't try with anyone." A few claim, "I don't have the money to entertain them in the way they entertained me."

All of these excuses miss the point. The purpose of

exchanging invitations is the building of relationships. It is not how it is done or the amount of money spent, but the time and love expressed. A single person can always invite people over for popcorn, pizza, spaghetti, or brownies. A person responsible for a large number of people can sponsor several buffets through the year. You can also take people to a restaurant or invite them out for a picnic. At the very least, you can have them over for coffee and cookies.

Just be certain to do something to return invitations, though. Not to do so is unkind and can cause lasting misunderstandings and hurt feelings.

Informality—the Key To Today's Relaxed Entertaining

The overall keynote of entertaining today is informality. This gives any hostess great freedom for a number of reasons. First of all, people are much more relaxed in an informal situation. They can dress more comfortably; there are fewer rules to worry about breaking; and guests feel less stress about unknown expectations.

Informality also tends to be less expensive. Simplicity in food, activities and dress tends to put the emphasis where it belongs—on the people. We can also entertain and share with others more frequently if we aren't worried about spending too much time or too much money on an event.

Informality tends to be less work. Many people want to entertain more often, but if they have to plan a five course dinner, polish silver, and cook for three days to prepare for it, they might not want to do it more than once or twice a year. Deciding to hold a potluck at your house, using paper plates, and inviting a group of friends to each bring a dish, makes for the kind of entertaining that can be done frequently and easily.

Here are some practical suggestions for entertaining informally.

(1) Informality is, first of all, a frame of mind embracing a relaxed, easy-going attitude toward the event and your guests. If you feel genuinely relaxed about what you are doing, if the people honestly mean more than the salad dressing, your guests will know it.

(2) One of the best aspects of entertaining informally is to serve your meal family style instead of in courses. Serving food in courses where first one gets an appetizer, then often a soup, then a main dish, then sometimes a salad, then fruit and cheese and/or dessert—all done on different dishes and with someone running back and forth to carry plates in and out—is the sort of production best left to restaurants.

It is much easier to simply place all the food on the table and encourage people to help themselves as they desire. The hostess isn't jumping up and down; the guests don't have to worry that someone is eating the soup so slowly that others are having to wait for the roast and so on. Family style creates a more pleasant, relaxed, enjoyable atmosphere. It is as easy to do as a buffet, but much more comfortable and more conducive to conversation among the guests.

To serve a typical dinner party family style, you may want to put simple appetizers in the living room area for your guests to enjoy as they arrive. When it is time for dinner, slip into the kitchen. Have the beverages, butter, salt, pepper and any necessary condiments already on the table. The main dish, then, can be taken out of the oven and placed in a serving basket that can sit right on the table. Place any vegetables or side dishes in similar containers. Put the bread on the bread board or in a basket; remove the salad from the refrigerator and place it on the table. Then call your guests to the table. It couldn't be easier.

(3) For entertaining a large number of people, paper plates and a buffet serving line are always appropriate. If you have them, the wicker trays that guests can place all their eating implements as well as a cup upon are especially useful.

In Addition to Informality

Though as a general rule an informal style will characterize most of your entertaining, there are times when you will want to make an event very special. A graduation, a wedding, an anniversary, a farewell, an appreciation dinner, any of these times call for special celebration.

Rather than courses, family style is still the best way to serve the meal, but there are a number of things you can do to make an event special.

(1) Ask your guests to dress up. Special clothes do add a festive air to any occasion.

(2) Dress up your table by using your china, silver, and white linens. If you don't own these items, borrow or rent them for special occasions. Renting is not usually costly and is sometimes much easier and far less expensive than owning items you might only want to use once or twice a year. Candles, fresh flowers, and silver serving pieces will also add to the festive air.

(3) Do special little things. Have place cards; announce, "this is a special dinner for our guest of honor," or make a truly spectacular dessert.

Specific Christian Concerns

If Christians are honest, we must realize that our faith, in addition to its spiritual implications, has placed us in somewhat of a special subculture in our present day world. Because of this, there are certain concerns in the whole area of manners which are important. Below are an assortment of some personal observations and suggestions.

(1) The Lord commands His children to invite those who cannot repay them to social events, and at least some of our entertaining should be for the purpose of ministry. All of it should be done from a heart of love for others. The Christian's invitation list should be a matter of much prayer for sensitivity from the Lord. In many churches single parents would give anything for a family to invite them for a meal, and for the father to perhaps take fatherless sons for an outing. The elderly often do not have their families living near them; the handicapped find people are embarrassed to be around them. People who are new to a church or community might long for a meal with friendly people who can answer their questions.

(2) When entertaining people who do not attend church, some specifically Christian actions, such as saying grace, can be embarrassing to people who don't practice it. This is especially true if nothing is said and suddenly half the table closes their eyes and bows their heads just as someone else is innocently reaching for the salad. The way I handle this situation is, as soon as I sit down, I fold my hands and say, "It is our custom at mealtime to thank God for our food. Would you please join us while I (or someone else) say grace."

This little statement works very well because people know exactly what is going to happen. Using the statement, "it is our custom," makes it sound less like those who don't normally say grace are sinful pagans. It has been interesting also to note the response of many of my non-Christian friends. Saying grace in a noncondemning, comfortable way has led many of them, later in the meal, to ask questions about God or the church. It is also interesting that now, when I am invited to their homes for a meal, they usually ask me to say grace for them.

The little phrase, "it is our custom," is also a useful introduction for many kinds of Christian behavior your guests may not be familiar with. For example:

● "It is our custom to go to church on Sundays. We would love to have you go with us while you are staying at our home."

● "It is our custom to rest and spend time with our family on Sunday afternoon."

Statements such as these are endless. If the person wants to know why something is your custom, you can then give them a spiritual explanation. The Bible says that the people heard Jesus gladly and that all sorts of people were comfortable around Him. That same attitude and atmosphere should be our goal.

4

CREATING THE SETTING FOR HOSPITALITY

In the tenth century, preparing for a party consisted of spreading fresh straw on the floor of the banquet hall. If possible, fresh herbs were added so they would release their fragrance as people walked across the straw. The table service consisted of large slabs of bread upon which the meat was placed. The hostess didn't have to worry about silverware, because the only thing used was a knife and everyone brought their own. Clean up was easy. The dogs took care of the bones and other scraps that were tossed to the floor, and the gravy soaked pieces of bread were distributed to the poor.

Things certainly have changed since then, haven't they?

Though it may have been simpler back then to just spread out the straw, it is certainly more fun to plan various ways to decorate our homes and tables as we entertain the people we love. Whether you live in a tiny apartment, or a huge house, whether you have a corner in the kitchen or a large formal dining room, whether you have a card table covered with checked gingham or a ten foot oak table—there are a multitude of enjoyable and interesting things you can do to make the setting for your hospitality fun.

Sometimes the setting of the party creates not only great fun at the time, but also great memories later. I will never forget when Vicki gave a party and had everyone dress in Medieval clothing. She emptied out two rooms of her house, actually put straw on the floors and borrowed skins to put on the walls. Debby organized a dinner in an Early Church theme for her youth group by putting tables on the floor. The kids sat on pillows and dressed like Romans. A formal dinner party for a military group was held in Ann's house. She rented small tables and had them decorated with flowers and ribbons in the squadron's colors. The variations and themes for parties are limited only by your imagination.

This chapter is a potpourri of ideas collected from friends, reading, observation and lots of experience in many situations over the years. Pick and choose what is useful for you. Alter ideas; combine them; store them away in your memory for just the right occasion.

Ideas For Your House

You don't need to confine special decorating ideas to just the centerpiece on the table. When you have guests, there are a variety of little things you can do throughout the house to say *welcome*. You may not want to do them for every dinner party, but for special occasions keep some of the following ideas in mind.

(1) Decorate your front door. Balloons, a wreath, a sign that says "welcome," all can get your event off to a good start.

(2) An arrangement of flowers by the sink says "welcome" in the bathroom. Guest soap is nice and so are guest towels.

Unfortunately, many people aren't quite sure if they are really supposed to use guest towels—especially if they are embroidered or of a fancy variety. One solution by a very gracious hostess was to have a little pile of guest hand towels in a plain color by her sink. Then on the floor, she had a little wicker basket with a slightly crumpled hand towel in it. This gave guests permission to use a fresh towel and then to toss it in the basket.

(3) Flowers or other arrangements can be used on the coffee table, a table in the foyer, or on a ledge in the kitchen. They need not be elaborate, but they do communicate that something special is happening. For children's parties or casual get-togethers, balloons all over the house are festive and fun.

(4) Lighting is very important to any occasion. Be sure you have enough light so people can see the setting clearly. But when you sit down to eat, you may want to lower the lights over the table. A dimmer switch is nice for this.

Of course one of the nicest ways to illuminate a party is with candles. Candles can be used on the table as a centerpiece or they can be placed all around the room. Here are some additional ideas for using candles.

● Don't feel you have to purchase expensive candles. The plain white ones found in the hardware store are great when you use a large quantity of them. So are inexpensive votive candles.

● Be original in your use of candleholders. Cut out the center of an apple for a nice fall centerpiece. You can also use various squashes or other firm fruits. Or, use a variety of candleholders of the same material, but that do not match each other, such as different brass candleholders or a collection of wooden spool candleholders.

● Candles set on or in front of mirrors magnify the

enjoyment and the light. One idea is to place an inexpensive mirror in the bottom of a wicker tray and then set votive candles on it. Place the tray on a coffee or side table to illuminate part of a room.

● Be sure to always put something below the candles to catch the drips. Even the best candles may drip some wax if there is a breeze or after burning for several hours. Here again a mirror or a platter is perfect. To clean it, you simply let the wax harden and scrape it off, or place it in warm water.

Specific Items For Hospitality

Dishes, linens, centerpieces, flowers—the homes of some individuals contain whole rooms filled with these items. You may only have a drawer or a kitchen cabinet full, but you can still prepare a lovely party and a beautiful table. Especially today, you no longer have to think only in terms of pure white linen, fine china and silver. You can use everything from colored sheets topped with colored paperware to center-pieces made from fresh vegetables or old toys.

As you think about entertaining, there are two principles to keep in mind. First of all, think about your style of entertaining. Do you primarily entertain informally or formally or a bit of both? If you never have a formal dinner, it is foolish to keep your eye out for old silver serving pieces. Sturdy country stoneware and baskets may be more what you will enjoy and use.

Second, have a basic color scheme in mind as you look for items for your party settings. This doesn't mean everything has to be in the exact same color, but they should coordinate. For example, my china has a green and gold pattern. I love Depression glass serving pieces, but I only collect green ones even though there are many other attractive colors. My stoneware is tan and brown and all baskets look great with it. With these limitations in mind, no matter how much I might like a pale rose glass bowl, I know it just wouldn't work for me.

If you don't have any dishes and want to find some, keep in mind the color scheme of the room in which you will do most of your decorating. A dining room with tiny Colonial pink flowers in the wallpaper would probably not look very good with geometric black dishes.

Know your style. Decide on your colors, and then begin to look around. Scout garage sales, secondhand stores and auctions for treasures to decorate your table. Look at remnant tables and linen sales. Below are some ideas on what to look for and how to use your finds.

Dishes and Flatware

When entertaining casually, you will probably want stoneware or pottery dishes. For more formal occasions, you may want to add china. In addition to these traditional selections, here are some other ideas for how to set your table.

(1) If you want china, but either don't want to spend a large amount of money on a new pattern or you want something a bit different, look around at antique stores, garage sales and second-hand stores. You can often find nearly complete sets of wonderful old china. Sometimes the pattern is a little bit faded, but it is lovely just the same.

Another idea that looks charming and can be put together for very little cost is to set a table with a variety of old china plates. Collect them as you can, assembling a potpourri of individual pieces you enjoy. You can also collect a variety of old silver or silverplate pieces in this way. If you use these with an old lace tablecloth, it creates a lovely setting.

(2) In addition to china, you can also find sets of old stoneware. Some of the brightly colored plates and sets from the fifties fit perfectly into today's contemporary decorating schemes. You might ask relatives or friends if they have any old dishes they aren't using. Sometimes someone else's castoffs are a perfect set of dishes for entertaining.

(3) As with the selection of nice china, don't feel everything has to match. If possible, you should stay with the same sort of dinnerware or in the same or coordinated color family; but nothing is wrong with four brown plates and four yellow plates at the same table.

(4) Keep your eye out for interesting serving pieces. Here again, they don't have to match the china or stoneware pattern as long as they are similar in texture and pattern. To use with my brown and cream stoneware, I have a selection of various handthrown pottery pieces in different brown tones, baskets and brown glassware from Mexico. As I mentioned earlier, to go with my green and gold china, I have a variety of green Depression glass serving pieces.

(5) At antique, secondhand, and similar stores, you can often find a variety of nice serving spoons and forks for very low prices. It is so nice to have enough large spoons and forks for serving, and this is a good way to accumulate them.

(6) One of the best all around solutions to a choice of dinnerware is to select a good quality, classic style of white stoneware. You can dress it up, play it down and use any sort of linens or table decorations with it. If you entertain frequently and like to entertain in a variety of ways, this choice is perfect.

Linens

Years ago, only pure white lace or damask linen was considered proper for your table. Fortunately today, we have a much wider choice. Imagination instead of tradition is what is valued in table settings. Below is a selection of ideas to get you started.

(1) In terms of traditional linens, take advantage of semi-annual white sales and other linen sales when you can get nice tablecloths and napkins for a fraction of their original price. Try to purchase special holiday linens just after the holidays. For example, Christmas tablecloths, table runners, napkins, and assorted items such as candles and centerpieces are at least half price at that time. Similar sales take place after other major holidays such as Thanksgiving, Valentine's Day and Easter.

(2) While you are in the linen section, look at some of the new sheet sets. One large sheet can be used to make both a tablecloth and some napkins. You can find sheets in almost any color and pattern imaginable. Another item to look for is small guest towels—they make great napkins.

Calico and country style handkerchiefs can also be used as napkins. Gingham, old pieces of printed or denim fabrics, and other fabric remnants can be cut up to make napkins.

(3) Use old quilts as tablecoverings, especially for a buffet table. You can top them with doilies for additional interest.

(4) When looking at the remnant table in your fabric store, consider getting enough material to make a contrasting table runner. There may not be enough material in any one piece to make a complete tablecloth or set of napkins, but many fabrics will work well for this added touch. For example,

plaid cottons in red and green are great for the holidays. Any sort of gold or silver or other metallic cloth makes exciting table runners; drapery material hung over a round table looks quite elegant. Rough linen and woven fabrics are perfect with a table setting featuring baskets and stoneware.

(5) Foreign import shops are another great source of table setting ideas. Indonesian batiks, Indian gauze fabrics, and straw placemats are only the beginning of ideas for unique tablecoverings.

(6) In addition to complete tablecloths, don't forget the usefulness of placemats. On any wood or glass table, they can be used without a tablecloth and others may be used with a tablecloth. I have a calico set I use on wood and a set of ivory lace ones that I use on white linen. I also have a raffia set that goes on wood with basket serving pieces for buffet serving.

Centerpieces and Table Decorations

Linens and tableware are the essentials, but centerpieces and table decorations are what often define an event as a celebration.

Your choice of what to use as a centerpiece can range from the ultra simple to super extravagant. I often enjoy using a flowering African violet or a small collection of garden flowers for a simple setting. But once, for a reception of 600 at a local television station premiere, I made a six-foot long centerpiece at the main table from gold-sprayed vegetables and white silk flowers. Both extremes and anything in between are fun and add immeasurably to a party.

Almost anything can be used as a centerpiece, rearranged, combined with something else, even spray-painted. Below are some ideas for centerpieces and table decorations, but

46

again, let these ideas just be the starting point of inspiration for you.

(1) A pile of presents can be used as a centerpiece in a number of ways. You can wrap empty boxes in paper appropriate to any occasion. You might try bright colors for a birthday party; pile them up with lots of balloons attached, or wrap small boxes in silver or gold and place in a crystal bowl for a holiday party. You can also wrap prizes for games, which is nice for a children's party. A variety of small gifts for the guest of honor, such as a variety of small kitchen items for a bridal shower, can be placed in a basket where it serves as a centerpiece for the duration of the party, and then is presented as a gift at the end.

(2) For children's parties, baby showers, and so on, a teddy bear, a doll or several different toys work well as a centerpiece. Or, you can get a group of interesting, but broken toys from secondhand stores and create an attractive centerpiece. An assortment of toys can also be spray painted to coordinate with the theme and color scheme of the party. For instance, for a baby boy's shower, pile together an assortment of little cars, building blocks, et cetera, and spray paint them blue.

(3) Various kinds of fresh vegetables make wonderful centerpieces. Broccoli, artichokes, eggplants, pumpkins, and squash—either a basket all of one kind or an assortment that is color coordinated—work great. And, the shape of the vegetables is fantastic. You could spray paint some broccoli black to go with a very contemporary setting or artichokes white for a winter party. Gold spray paint adds a Midas touch to any setting.

(4) Fresh fruits also work well. Apples and walnuts are a nice combination; lemons and limes are lovely. A centerpiece of fresh fruit always looks attractive and can double as a

buffet dessert if you wish.

(5) Several houseplants in small, attractive containers can be used for many centerpieces. African violets are perfect. Other plants that are useful include primroses, Swedish ivy, English ivy, shamrocks, begonias, coleus, small cactus, etc. You can grow them in little pottery pots, baskets or some of the terra cotta animal planters that are now popular. If you have little plants like this, you can always pick one, flank it with a couple of votive candles and even the most casual lunch becomes more special. In addition, if you wish to make a larger centerpiece for a buffet setting, you can combine several small plants with flowers or other centerpiece settings such as baskets of fruits or vegetables.

(6) Dried flowers also make attractive decorations and you can gather many of these yourself in the fall. Aspen leaves combined with dried flowers, a bit of wood and wild rose hips have made an attractive centerpiece for my fall table for the past several months. Dried flower arrangements tend to look better if you stick with only one, or at the most, three kinds of flowers. Too large of a variety makes it look like just a handful of weeds. Just one kind, say aspen leaves in a pottery pot, dried Queen Anne's Lace in an old basket, wild rose hips in old pewter—any of these types of combinations are attractive. Just be sure to use plants that are thoroughly dried. Don't bring them in freshly cut when their pollen could cause allergy problems.

(7) Certain filler items are handy to have on hand when making centerpieces. For example, a bunch of baby's breath is always nice to fill out a floral centerpiece. For a centerpiece made of anything from colored toys to vegetables, tuck in some baby's breath and anything is softened.

Ribbons are also great to finish out a centerpiece. You can purchase ribbon in varying widths from floral supply houses and hobby shops. You can make ribbon loops in centerpieces and flower arrangements, and table runners coming out from the centerpiece. You can string ribbon from lighting fixtures; you can tie bows on serving pieces and furniture; you can combine ribbon with balloons and string balloons from them.

(8) Balloons do make great party centerpieces, and can be combined with almost anything.

Flowers

Flowers are, without a doubt, one of God's most wonderful delights, and they are one of the most perfect of all centerpieces and special occasion decorations. Decorating with flowers need not be difficult or expensive. In addition to a good pair of scissors for cutting your flowers, you just need a bit of imagination and bravery, and some of the hints below.

(1) You will need a few basic flower arranging supplies. The most important one being green florist foam. This can be purchased at floral supplies and hobby shops. Rather than styrofoam, get the variety that has a very fine texture and to which you add water before putting in the flowers. This foam must, of course, be used in a waterproof container. It will keep the flowers standing upright as well as well watered.

The containers for flower arranging can be anything from standard vases to baskets, toys, pottery, hollowed-out pumpkins and squash, old china teacups, and silver. Florist and hobby shops sell baskets for flower arranging that have a plastic lining and these are quite useful and easy to use. I have also found some great containers for flower arranging at restaurant supply houses. On a discard table, I once found some little white china teapots with their lids missing and small black china creamers. Have a place to keep these kinds of things when you find them. Not only do they make distinctive centerpieces for parties but, if you wish, you can always give the completed centerpiece to the guest of honor to take home.

(2) Once you have the basic supplies, you need to find a place to purchase flowers. You can make very simple and attractive arrangements using just a few flowers, as few as 3-5 will do, and by adding additional filler such as baby's breath and a few bits of greenery. Many supermarkets sell flowers, and you might visit your local florist to see how much individual flowers and a bit of greenery cost. You can also use dried baby's breath with fresh flowers. It is often cheaper to purchase and easier to keep on hand than the fresh.

To make a simple arrangement:

● Put the florist's foam in the bottom of a waterproof container about four to five inches across.

● Wet the foam with water.

● Take three to seven flowers—carnations, roses, lilies, mums, whatever—and put them into the foam, having cut them into lengths of about six inches.

● Add some greenery. If possible, use fern from the florist's. If you don't have any, cut off a sprig of English or Swedish ivy from your houseplants.

● Fill in the arrangement with baby's breath.

This process, which takes only a few minutes, makes a lovely, simple arrangement. Once you have made it and you see how easy it is to arrange your own fresh flowers, you can then attempt all sorts of variations with two or three kinds of flowers, using different kinds of greenery and fillers.

If you wish, you can use silk flowers instead of fresh flowers. Follow the same basic instructions except, of course, don't wet the florist's foam. You can also get some lovely effects combining silk flowers with fresh flowers. A simple book on flower arranging will give you many additional hints and ideas.

(3) With flowers, you can never go wrong using all one color or a mass of all the same flowers. For example, an assortment of all white flowers in a silver or crystal container is always elegant. A bouquet of daffodils is lovely for a spring luncheon or bridal shower. Four or five yellow mums in a rust colored pottery pot looks great for a fall buffet.

(4)   If you don't want to arrange flowers, you can use pots of flowering plants such as spring bulbs, geraniums and miniature roses. Special season greens such as holly at Christmas or pussy willow twigs in the spring also work well.

Keep on loving each other as brothers. Do not forget to entertain strangers, for by so doing some people have entertained angels without knowing it.

Hebrews 13:1-2

5

ENTERTAINING IS MORE THAN EATING

You've planned the menu, the decorations are decided, the guest list is complete—but all of a sudden you think, "whatever will my guests do when dinner is over?"

The question usually answers itself if the people know each other well. Conversation flows naturally as friends share common interests and concerns. But, not every instance of hospitality includes just people who know each other well. Sometimes it is intentionally made up of strangers whom you want to get to know better; friends from various groups you want to introduce to each other; newcomers you want to make feel welcome; out-of-town guests you want to introduce to old friends. In all of these and similar situations, structuring your time together will enable people to have a more enjoyable time and get to know one another better.

This can be done in a variety of ways from a completely structured party where everything from the introductions to the farewell is planned out in advance, to simple conversation starters the hostess has in the back of her mind to use if the occasion calls for it, to a few games to suggest if the time seems to lag. No matter what you do, a primary principle of entertaining is to tailor the activities to the needs and desires of the guests. Activities and games should always be secondary to people. If everyone is talking comfortably and enjoying the fellowship, making guests quit talking to play a game can be self-defeating.

Below are a number of ideas from the simplest to ones that take a bit more planning. Use whatever you think your occasion and your guests require.

Conversation Starters

Sometimes people just need to know a little more about each other to give them lots to talk about. Structured conversation is useful for this. Have someone ask a series of questions which everyone answers with their own personal facts, opinions or memories. This sort of activity is excellent with a group of people who don't know each other well. For example, a new members get-together at church, or a new study group has just formed. These groups need some sort of structured discussion to get them talking to each other. It is sometimes interesting to sit around the dinner table with friends you have known for a long time and share in a similar way. You'll be amazed at what you can learn about people you thought you knew well.

To begin, the hostess announces that the group is going to take some time to get to know each other better, or makes a similar statement. She asks a question and then everyone goes around the table or room and answers it. The questions can and should be very simple and non-threatening. For example:

- Where were you born and where did you graduate from high school?

- Did you have a pet when you were a kid? If you did, what was its name and what did you like about it?
- What was the best thing that happened to you this week?
- What is your best memory about your grandparents? Or grade school teachers? Or Christmas as a child?
- What was the best gift you ever received?
- Where would you go if you could travel anywhere in the world? Why?
- "Most" questions are always useful, such as: When in your life were you most proud of an accomplishment? Most embarrassed? Most happy? Most sad?

If the group is composed of people with one similar characteristic, you can tailor the questions to fit that group. For example:

(1) If it is all married couples, ask them how they met, or what was their favorite anniversary present, or how the husband proposed, or what their wedding flowers were.

(2) If all young mothers, ask for their greatest cute kid story in two minutes or less, greatest toilet training disaster, greatest food mess.

(3) If all Christians, ask when everyone came to know the Lord, what is the most comforting thing about Christianity to them, the most troublesome, who they would like to meet in heaven.

After you have asked a number of these questions, you might have each one present think up a question to ask the group.

(4) A variation on this activity was used at a church new members dinner. Each person was asked to make two statements about themselves, one was to be true and the other was to be false. The group then had to vote on which was which and the results were fascinating. Somehow in that game, people had the courage to say things about themselves

they never would have told someone spontaneously.

For additional ideas on questions to ask, look at a copy of the *Ungame*. It is a board game in which the players move around the board and select cards which require them to answer all kinds of questions about each other. It is a good game to play with four to six, but for a less intense version, just use some of their questions. Some relational Bible studies also have questions such as these. Spend some time looking around your local Christian bookstore for ones you might use.

Costume and Theme Parties

While structured conversation might be one of the simplest of planned activities for a group get-together, costume and theme parties are one of the most complex. At the same time, they provide the context for all the activities you might need because you can organize everything from food to games to decorations around the theme. Halloween is the obvious time for a costume party, but below are some additional ideas.

(1) Have a theme party centering around a country and emphasize the missionary work of that country. Prepare native food and have a speaker from there. If complete costumes would be too complex, just make hats or some other article of clothing from that country.

(2) Have an evening of "Living Bible Lessons." To do this, have everyone dress in costumes from Bible times. (Old bathrobes or sheets wrapped around a person do fine.) Have two or three people in more complex costumes impersonate people like David and Nathan, or Daniel and his three friends, or Peter, James and John, or Paul and Timothy. Have them remain in character throughout the evening and

give some sort of presentation. For example:

● David could talk about how he wanted to build the temple, how it was the dream of his heart, and what he felt when Nathan told him God did not want him to do it. Nathan could share how difficult it was for him to go to his king and tell him that God did not want him to fulfill his dream— especially after he had already told him it was all right to do it.

● Paul could tell how dangerous his journeys were and Timothy could share what he, as a young person, learned from them.

● Peter could tell how his life was changed after Jesus rose from the dead, how surprised he was that someone who denied the Lord to a servant girl, now had the courage to stand up before multitudes to proclaim Him.

These sorts of parties are really a kind of living history and can work especially well with young people. Have the main characters study their parts well. The research alone will be both fun and enlightening. Then have them answer questions and share in character for the entire evening. This is an excellent way to have the Bible literally come alive in a way many have never before experienced.

(3) A similar, but somewhat different theme party would be a "Living Church History Party." This may take a bit more research and work, but select a time out of church history—perhaps the Reformation or an early frontier period of missionary work. Your main character might be Martin Luther just as he finishes Romans or his early debates. Or, you could be one of the first missionaries to preach to the Indians.

Service and Project Parties

Quilting bees and barn raisings—our ancestors knew how to combine fun and work that would benefit everyone. Even today, parties where we combine fun and work that can help others are a great response to the command to "make the most of our time." Below are some ways to do this:

(1) Find a nursing home, a home for children, or a shelter for battered women in your community. Then find out if there are some special foods they need or would enjoy. For example, almost everybody enjoys homemade cookies—and not just at Christmas time. Get a group of friends together to bake and decorate cookies, and then take them to the home. You can have other food events, too, such as breadmaking, jam making, soup and casserole making.

Vary the food project based upon the skills and ages of the participants. Older grade school kids through teens can all decorate and package cookies; experienced cooks might want to make casseroles to stock a church pantry or give to shut-ins.

(2) Your group can also make other holiday items such as decorated Easter eggs or Christmas cookies for children in the hospital during these seasons.

(3) Women's groups can have old-fashioned sewing bees to make layettes and clothes for pregnancy services in your city. Or you can mend and re-condition clothes for secondhand shops. Many missionary groups can also use clothes, blankets and other items that need some repair.

(4) Men can get together to make toys, fix baby furniture or do house repair work for the elderly or disabled.

(5) Another way to help the elderly or disabled is for any group (from teens to singles to married couples) to do odd jobs, yard work, or painting on one Saturday a month. Then

they can meet at someone's house for a chili or other simple supper afterward.

(6) Another variation on this kind of party is the "How-to Party." At this kind of gathering, someone with a particular skill or talent offers to teach others how to do it for free. Why pay a professional to teach you how to do something when we all have talents we can share with one another? Gather a group of friends in a home or central meeting place such as a church basement and learn to do things like:

- prepare tax returns
- simple car repairs
- make bread
- can pickles
- easy watercolor painting
- refinish furniture
- arrange flowers
- simple woodworking
- simple home repairs
- financial management

Organized Games

Though we normally think of games as fun things to do during our recreation times, we must remember that games are not neutral. Especially for children, games are also learning times. And, for any age, games emphasize the values that are important to us. Games tell people whether competition or creative fun is more important; whether our imagination is a gift from God or a tool for evil.

With these cautions in mind, be very careful of the games you select for your children and guests. If you haven't had a chance to do so recently, take some time to visit your local Christian bookstore and look at some of the exciting, creative and fun games put out by the various Christian publishing houses. Some of the things you will find include:

(1) A large selection of Bible games. Trivia games are tremendously popular and people enjoy the challenge of

remembering all sorts of bits and pieces of knowledge. What could be better than to stimulate an in-depth knowledge of the Bible and to have fun while doing it?

(2) *Dragonraid* is a beautifully illustrated fantasy game for all ages that teaches Bible memory and Christian discipleship, while providing the participants with a fun time.

(3) *Ungame*, already mentioned but a very creative way to learn more and enjoy more of each other.

(4) In addition, there are numerous Christian entertainment products for children such as Bible character puppets, VCR tapes, and audio tapes. Try some of these at parties for children of all ages.

Make-a-Memory Games

Many parties celebrate significant events in one's life—the birth of a child, graduation from school, a wedding, an anniversary, leaving a place, starting a new career. We mark these times with joyous festivities. But in addition to the event itself, we often want to give our guest of honor something by which he can remember the event. This means you can not only provide a fun activity for the occasion, but you can also supply a treasured heirloom for your honored guest.

There are many ways to "make a memory." The important thing is to have the project finished at the end of the party for the guest of honor to take with him.

For any age, get a photo album, a Polaroid camera and some index cards. Take a picture of each person at the party, either alone or with the guest of honor. Then on the index card have them write something like:

- fondest memory of their friend
- best advice they can give

● dreams they want to come true for them
● how they will miss them
● anything else they want to say

Have each person read their advice to the guest of honor, then place the pictures and the cards in the album.

Variations of the Advice and Picture Memory

(1) For a new baby shower, take a picture of each guest and then have them write out one piece of advice, a life verse and prayer for the child, and one encouragement for the new mother when life becomes difficult. You could do a similar thing for a wedding shower.

(2) For the retirement of a pastor or other church worker, take pictures of families in the church and then have each family write out their most treasured memory of the person(s) retiring or leaving. For a memory album like this, you could also plan ahead and enclose pictures of the church and various events in the past that would be meaningful to the person honored.

<6> SPECIAL KINDS OF HOSPITALITY

Hospitality doesn't always come in tidy little packages of dinner parties for six or open houses for twenty where you have the perfect setting and situation. Hospitality often takes place in a variety of unique situations and involves people of all ages. This chapter discusses some of these situations with a variety of ideas on how to handle them.

Entertaining As a Single

If you aren't regularly practicing hospitality as a single person, you are depriving yourself of a great source of joy and satisfaction. "He who would have friends must show himself friendly," the Bible tells us in Proverbs 18:24, and one of the best ways to be friendly is to practice hospitality.

You don't need a partner, a home of your own, a large dining room or fancy dishes and linens to entertain. You only need a heart that wants to share with other people. Think of possibilities and develop your own successful and delightful entertaining style. Here are some ideas.

(1) Evaluate your situation and then develop one or two kinds of entertaining that suits it. For example, if you live in a very small place, learn how to give a tea party for four to six people. If you live in an apartment or townhouse complex with a large meeting room, you might have potlucks or open house buffets in it.

(2) Once you have selected the kind of entertaining you want to do, think of a few things you feel comfortable making. You don't have to master the entire art of cooking to be a successful hostess. You can be known for your great stew, your fantastic chili, or for the super nachos you make. Or maybe, when everyone gets together and brings over pizza, you make a delicious pie for dessert.

(3) As a single it is easy to think that people must invite you over for holidays, Sunday dinners or special occasions. Instead of waiting for invitations, *you* can be the initiator; *you* can organize holiday gatherings, *you* can invite people for dinner.

(4) As a twist on hospitality for a single, you can follow the example of my friend Jeanie. One Sunday afternoon she called and said she wanted to spend the evening with my husband and me. She wondered if it would be okay if she brought over a take-out chicken dinner for all of us. It sounded great to me, so I set the table with paper plates, made tea and we had a great time together without anyone having to do lots of extra work.

(5) Most of all, value yourself and your home. You are unique. You are loved by God. You are special. And all of those characteristics you can share through your own individualized, gracious hospitality.

Entertaining At a Restaurant

There are times in one's life when you are either unwilling or unable to entertain at home. Perhaps you are simply tired of cooking, still want to share a meal with friends, but can't bear spending the necessary hours in the kitchen to do it. Perhaps, for some reason, your kitchen isn't functional; you are remodeling or something essential like the oven isn't working too well. Perhaps you just want to share a restaurant you enjoy with friends. Whatever the occasion, there are times you will want to share your hospitality at a place different than your home. Here are a few hints on how to do it graciously.

(1) If at all possible, never take guests to a restaurant with which you are not completely familiar. Know the menu, the food, the people who work there, what days certain items are on special, the chef's night off, or any other important detail that could spell disaster for you if you are unaware of it.

(2) When you invite your guests, make sure they know you are treating them. It is quite important how you word this so there is no misunderstanding. A statement such as, "we would like to have you join us for dinner at such and such restaurant on Friday night," leaves it unclear as to whether the people you ask to join you are to pay their own way or not. Instead, you should say, "Paul and I would like to treat you and Jim to dinner at a favorite restaurant of ours on Friday. Can you join us?"

(3) Have your guests join you for appetizers or a small snack at your house prior to going out. For a recent dinner at a restaurant, I first had guests over for nachos. A simple snack such as this takes the edge off everyone's hunger, and allows some time for a little relaxation and conversation. If you then go to dinner at a Mexican restaurant and the dinner

is not served immediately, everyone is much more at ease.

(4) You should, of course, make reservations ahead of time and, if possible, reserve a table or area in the restaurant that you know is pleasant. If the occasion is an extra special one, you can always order flowers and have them placed at the table, or pre-order a special dessert or main dish.

(5) At the restaurant, make some menu suggestions. This accomplishes two things. First of all, it helps guests make a selection from an unfamiliar menu, and second, it sets a price range in a tactful way.

(6) Be as discreet as possible about paying the bill. If it is a restaurant where you are well-known and you trust them, you can sign a charge slip when you come in or ahead of time, and the bill need never appear at the table. At the least, you should ask the waiter to give the check to you and handle it quietly.

(7) If you entertain regularly at a certain restaurant, be sure to let the management know how much you appreciate their service. Tell them how much it means to you to be able to bring your guests and know that all of you will have an excellent meal and a pleasant time.

Entertaining With and For Children

Children are a very special part of entertaining and should be considered whether or not you have children of your own. Below are a few hints if you do not have children and have friends who do. There are also some hints on involving your own children in entertaining.

If you do not have children of your own, but your guests do:

(1) Decide ahead of time what areas of your home are off

limits to children. For example, the living room and recreation room may be fine, but your study with a computer in it may not be. Be kind but firm about your decision when you inform both the parents and the children of your house rules. If possible, shut the door to a restricted area and lessen the temptation for your younger guests.

(2) Be realistic about your expectations concerning children. They are not little adults. They are children and the things that interest adults do not necessarily interest them. It is only considerate to have on hand a variety of toys or games.

For many years I have had a toybox in the guest room filled with all sorts of toys and books (collected as cast-offs from friends or from secondhand stores). Children who visited knew they could always go to the toybox and play with whatever they found. The only rule was they had to put everything back into the toybox when they left. Of course you need to be sure you have no dangerous or messy toys such as crayons in a toybox such as this. Various stuffed animals or dolls, simple blocks or other construction items, puzzles, trucks and cars, board games for older children, an assortment of books—all of these items are fine. You will find you don't need fancy or complicated items. Children are masters of imagination and just enjoy playing with someone else's things.

If you are having a dinner party and there are a number of children, if at all possible set up their own table. If it is a casual dinner, the children could even have a "picnic" where they could eat on a blanket with paper plates while their parents eat at the table.

For your own children, involve them as much as possible in the entertainment process. They are never too young to learn how to prepare for a party even if they simply straighten the pillows on the sofa. Have a good attitude about entertaining; give your children the gift of seeing you practice hospitality as a joyful act of sharing your home and your love. In addition to teaching them a good attitude, you will teach them the practical aspects of hospitality. This will, of course, vary with their ages and ability levels, but the suggestions below will give you some ideas you can adapt.

(1) Ask them who the family should invite for Sunday dinner. They may think of a family in their Sunday School class you might not, or someone they know is lonely whom you may have missed.

(2) Involve them in the menu planning process. Not only will this teach them about hospitality, but they will also learn about food and nutrition in a way that is more fun than just planning regular dinners for the family.

(3) Have them help make decorations and help put them up. They should also get to help take them down and assist in other related clean-up chores.

(4) According to age, assign them duties as hosts and hostesses.

I recently observed an excellent example of parental coaching on how to be a good host when, along with some other couples, my husband and I had dinner at a friend's house. There were only two children present. The child of the family at whose house we were and Jeff, age 10. Chad, age 12, invited Jeff, the guest, to have a soft drink with him and to see his room while the adults had appetizers. After dinner Chad then invited Jeff to see his new computer game while the adults continued their conversation around the dinner table. He also asked Jeff if he would like another soft drink and was an absolutely delightful host to his young guest. I later complimented Chad's mother on the excellent manners of her son and she assured me that they had not happened by accident.

No matter how young children are, they can learn the concept of what it means to be a gracious host or hostess by observing their parents and by structured learning. There are several popular schools across the country where children are taught manners and how to act in social situations. Without sending children to these kinds of schools, parents can accomplish the same thing by having practice sessions at home privately. For example, father can come in the door and the child can offer to take his coat. Children can also practice bringing out appetizers, putting ice and beverages in glasses, or offering sugar and cream to guests with their coffee.

(5) Kids can also help in the kitchen. Karen, the mother of two delightful preteens, shared the following observations of what children enjoy and do well in the kitchen. I'll pass her ideas on to you.

● Kids love gadgets. Give them an egg slicer for egg salad, a garlic press for guacamole, an apple slicer for apples and honey.

● Miniature foods are fun for kids to work with: party rye bread, muffins from small muffin pans, individual salad servings, and Cornish game hens which they see as "baby turkeys."

● Kids are great at assembly line projects like hors d'oeuvres. Put them to work making antipastos, stuffing celery or other vegetables, and building cheese logs.

● Children really enjoy foods with the shape of something familiar. Cook pancakes with ears to be Mickey Mouse; shape bread dough into animals; decorate gingerbread or cup cakes to look like members of the family or favorite friends.

In addition to the actual event, teach your children the

customs surrounding hospitality. Even a very young child can write a simple thank-you if his mother writes it out first and has the child copy it. Children can also learn to return invitations to parties they have attended; and they should be reminded to thank the parent who hosts a party they attend.

Hospitality To Internationals

Hospitality to foreigners is a very special way to practice hospitality because it combines both the sharing of hospitality and the opportunity to present Christ.

Missions has been an essential part of the Christian church since its earliest days. According to John Rantal, director of the church ministries division for International Students, Inc., "Half of the people of the world live in countries that forbid Christian missionaries."

International Students exists because of that situation, and they believe that America is a "modern Jerusalem." They use this analogy because in the days of the early church people from all over the world went to Jerusalem, heard about Christianity and from there took the message back to their home countries. Today, people from all over the world come to the United States for work or study.

According to ISI, 40,000 internationals live in Los Angeles, 17,000 in Boston, 35,000 in Washington, D.C. and 15,000 in Dallas. In addition to the sheer numbers, these people often have an influence far beyond the individuals because these are often either the future leaders of their nations or those who already occupy important positions. For example, Harvey Karlsen who worked with ISI in Boston said, "If I actually lived in Seoul, Korea, I could never even get an appointment with the lady who came to our house for

Bible Study each week." He went on to explain that she was a high level Korean government lawyer who was at Harvard as a visiting fellow. But what no amount of government influence could accomplish—for her to study the Bible and find the Savior—was accomplished by a concerned family who was kind to her.

Though ISI trains people in ways to minister to internationals, they give the general advice that Christians should simply be aware of those from other countries who live in their communities. There are many internationals on college campuses and in businesses. Once one is known, it is a very simple matter to include the person in family meals and holidays and to work on developing a friendship. John Rantal stated that the average American lives within 20-30 minutes of an international, but we think we have to go to another country to be a missionary. He emphasized that internationals are close to each of us and exercising hospitality toward them can be literally life-changing.

He told the story of a Sikh from India who came to America to study engineering. The Indian was befriended by a Christian couple and after two years of their hospitality he came to know Christ. "He returned to India," Rantal said, "with an engineering degree and a Bible." The Indian became an itinerant preacher and started more than 700 churches in India, Pakistan and Nepal.

7

EXTENDED HOSPITALITY

One day Elisha went to Shunem. And a well-to-do woman was there, who urged him to stay for a meal. So whenever he came by, he stopped there to eat. She said to her husband, "I know that this man who often comes our way is a holy man of God. Let's make a small room on the roof and put in it a bed and a table, a chair and a lamp for him. Then he can stay there whenever he comes to us."

II Kings 4:8-10

I can still remember when I first heard this story told. I was in a children's Sunday School class and the teacher recreated the story using flannelgraph pictures of a woman preparing a little room for her guest. As young as I was, I remember thinking her action was one of the kindest I had ever heard.

I still think it is. Practicing extended hospitality, sharing our home for a night, or a month, can be a Christian service and a witness of immeasurable worth and value. Pray and discuss with your family the possibility of extended hospitality as a family ministry. In our hurting and lonely world there is a great need for families to share their homes and hearts with either the temporarily or permanently homeless.

Should you decide you want to do this, here are some other situations you might want to consider in the practice of extended hospitality. These can be in addition to sharing with relatives and friends who happen to be in town, which is an art in itself to do graciously.

(1) Provide a guest room for a college student who goes to a college near you, but is far away from his or her home. Let the student know he/she is welcome to come any time, especially on weekends or for holidays to get away from dormitory living. At the same time, get to know some of their friends and invite them all over for an occasional meal.

(2) Have a room or even a guest cottage available to missionaries who are traveling through, are on fund raising trips, or are on a furlough. Let your church office know about your availability. You might also contact some other churches or your denominational headquarters.

(3) Contact your local Crisis Pregnancy Center. There is often a need for shepherding homes for single women who do not wish to have an abortion and need a place to stay until their child is born.

The list above can obviously be expanded. Look around and be aware of the needs of people and you'll find many uses for a guest room.

The Guest Room Itself

Once you have decided you would like to practice extended hospitality, here are some ideas on how to set up a guest room.

If you have a huge house with lots of extra space, it is simple to set up a room solely for the use of guests. Usually, however, most of us need to make our rooms serve double or triple duty and a guest room often fills many uses. Here are some ideas that can make this double function easier.

(1) First of all, don't select a room that is constantly used for something else. A recreation room that is sometimes used for television watching, a library where reading infrequently takes place, a closed-in porch that is used for occasional sewing—all of these work well. But don't choose a den, family room or any other area the family would be in and out of frequently. Constant family traffic makes a guest feel in the way.

(2) The most obvious piece of double duty furniture for the double duty guest room is, of course, a sofa bed. Be sure to get one that is both comfortable to sleep on and comfortable to sit on. Don't feel you have to purchase a brand new one, though, if you don't have one. Many secondhand and Goodwill stores have newly re-upholstered ones that are very nice. Check out the stores in your area.

(3) In addition to a place to sleep, you can put a small chest beside the bed to serve as an end table, night stand and clothes chest for guests. Don't forget to have a reading lamp and a clock on this table.

(4) Be sure to have a place for guests to hang their clothes. If you have an extra closet in that room, be sure part of it is empty and that there are extra coat hangers for your guests. If you don't have a closet, as at present we don't in our recreation/den room/guest room combination, use a coat tree or hang a clothing rack on the back of a door.

(5) Be sure there is a mirror in the room. You can combine this into the decor of a room easily. For example, I have a

mirror in a wooden frame along with some pictures hanging above a small wooden desk in the room I use for guests. The desk looks great in my normal use of the room and when guests arrive, they can use it to write letters or postcards or as a dressing table.

(6) In the bathroom your guests will be using, be sure to have supplies of toothpaste, hair spray, hand lotion, deodorant, shampoo, cream rinse, mouthwash and aspirin handy. An unopened toothbrush is good to keep on hand and extra bath oil or bubble bath is also a treat. Let your guests know these are for their use. Also show them where additional towels and washclothes are located.

(7) Other nice touches to include in a guest room are:
- A trash can in a convenient place.
- If you do have a little desk or other writing area, stock it with pen, pencils, paper, a few post cards and stamps.
- Put a selection of relatively current magazines and a daily newspaper in your guest room. Keep your eye out for publications from your Chamber of Commerce or any other publications of local interest or history and place them where your guests can read and enjoy them.
- Fresh flowers are always lovely. Even simple things like a few flowers from your garden, a group of flowering branches or fall leaves make a room special.
- A basket of fresh fruit, a little dish of candy, a basket of small packages of chips or nuts is a nice touch in a guest room also. A water carafe and glass are also appreciated.
- In one drawer it is nice to have a small sewing kit, shoe care items, and a clothes brush.
- Have a box of tissues handy.
- Remember to add other items for specific guests. If you know a college student who comes frequently likes a certain magazine, try to have it. If Aunt Amy loves

daisies, put a few in a vase for her. If someone is staying with you who is going through a particularly bad time, you can place encouraging Christian reading material in the room for them.

Food and Extended Hospitality

Don't feel you are on call twenty-four hours a day to serve as a short order cook when you have extended guests. If you want to make an extra nice meal or two that is fine, but your normal cooking will be most appreciated.

It is often easier for both you and your guests to have a supply of breakfast and lunch items and let guests know they can help themselves to these things at any time. This allows all of you to feel more relaxed. For example:

(1) For breakfast, have several beverages on the counter on a tray. Have instant coffee, creamer and sugar, a selection of both herb and regular tea, and some instant hot chocolate. Keep a large pot of water hot in a coffee maker not only at breakfast, but during the day, and your guests can be free to help themselves.

In addition to beverages, show them where the toaster, butter, bread and jam are located. Keep juice and milk available in the refrigerator. Small containers of yogurt are also nice to include in a selection such as this. In a convenient cupboard, have a selection of cold breakfast cereals and perhaps a few of the instant hot varieties. A handy bowl of fruit completes a selection that should satisfy every taste.

(2) For lunch you can also use a number of the breakfast items such as the milk, juice, hot beverages and fruit bowl. In addition, have a selection of sliced luncheon meats and

cheeses. Some packages of chips or sliced and cleaned vegetable pieces are good to have on hand also. A plate of cookies or brownies provides a sweet whenever someone wants one.

Cautions On Extended Hospitality

As important a ministry as extended hospitality can be, it is not without its dangers and concerns.

The first has to do with the care of your attitude as a hostess. Set limitations for yourself in your hospitality. You are providing a home, meals and care. Do not feel you have to entertain your guests every minute of their stay with you. Not only do people enjoy their own private time, but you will enjoy practicing hospitality much more if you don't feel you have to be constantly on duty. That is why you do things like having breakfast foods available for everyone to help themselves. If you feel you have to get up an hour early to make a fancy breakfast every day of the week, you can find yourself resenting your guests. On the other hand, if you all get your own toast and tea, you can really enjoy conversation with your friends in the morning.

If your guests are friends or relatives, don't feel you have to take every sightseeing trip with them. People enjoy exploring on their own with the proper preparation, and it will give you time to catch up on home and housework responsibilities. Also, don't overschedule your guests' time. Allow open time, time for sleeping in, and time to simply relax.

If your guests are more of a ministry situation, for instance a pregnant teenager living with you, sit down with your guest at the beginning and, as a family, go over house rules and responsibilities. Your guest should share in the work and the activities of the family, and should be accountable for her actions. If you have a frequent guest, such as a college student, he should understand that he is to clean his room after each use and that though his friends might be welcomed, he is not to bring them over unannounced. Sometimes it is difficult to discuss house rules, but if this is done honestly at the beginning of the guest's stay, it will make the entire time more pleasant and free of misunderstandings.

One final caution is important when you are considering extended hospitality as a ministry. Know your limitations and know the resources in your community for transient, borderline criminal, and mental illness problems. I learned this lesson the hard way a number of years ago. I have always had a guest room and it has been used by a multitude of people: missionaries, pregnant teens, college students, relatives, friends, all sorts of people.

One day, however, when I was taking a walk, I found a young woman literally wandering the streets near my house. I took her home and after a week or so of very bizarre behavior, my husband turned her over to the social services agency in our town. We were unable to handle her actions and were at a loss as to how to help. A short time later, we received a phone bill for $600.00 in long distance phone calls she had made from our phone when we were not home and, of course, we had to pay it.

The Lord requires our love and hospitality, but He also wants us to use discernment.

8

SPECIFIC PARTY SUGGESTIONS WITH MENUS

This book is filled with a multitude of ideas—sections on decorations, suggestions for activities and games, a collection of mouth watering recipes. But as helpful as all of these parts are, they can sometimes be a bit confusing. It is a little bit like an artist who has before him a marvelous palette of colors, a well-stretched white canvas, brushes of every shape and size and the perfect subject to paint—but who doesn't know where to start combining all of these elements into the perfect work of art.

If you feel like that when you approach the actual exercise of hospitality—a recipe looks good, that activity sounds nice, that table setting looks intriguing—but you don't know how to combine all of them into what you want to do, this chapter is for you. First of all, there is a review and some additional ideas on how to go about planning an event. Then specific types of hospitality will be discussed along with miscellaneous ideas and menus for each of them. After reading through them, you will have a better idea of what to do to make your hospitality the work of art you want it to be.

Cater Your Own Party

A little bit of objectivity is sometimes helpful when it comes to planning a hospitality event. To gain the needed objectivity, pretend that you are a professional caterer and plan the party that way. Look at it as a job to be accomplished as quickly, easily and successfully as possible. This will help you emphasize to yourself that planning is the key element of any successful occasion. Using your entertainment notebook, described in chapter 2, as a place to record each of these procedures, here are the various steps that should go into your planning.

(1) Decide on the purpose of the event, the approximate number of guests you wish to invite, and the date.

(2) Make your guest list and do the inviting. For all but the most formal occasions, you can do this by telephone. Be sure to give the date, time, address and directions if some guests are unfamiliar with where you live. Include information on whether the event is to be casual or dressy. Be clear whether or not children are included.

(3) Now plan your menu, taking into consideration the guidelines in chapter 9. Or, for a party for more than 25, see chapter 10. Also keep in mind the mood of the occasion, the tastes, and the preferences of your guests as you select the food to be served.

(4) Next, take an inventory of all the things you will need. See if you have them all on hand or will need to borrow or rent some. Be sure to include plates, serving bowls, flatware, linens. If renting glassware and plates, or in purchasing some of the attractive plastic and paper ones now available, plan on 1½ plates and glasses per guest.

(5) Decide on the decorations you want to use. See chapter 4 for ideas, but, in general, decide on what centerpiece you

will need, if you will use candles or not, and any additional decorations you might want to include. If you find you need to purchase some items, work out a budget and purchasing plan.

(6) One of the most important items to your peace of mind is a "To Do List." Once you have this made, you don't have to worry about forgetting to do something. If it is all on paper, you just have to consult your list and check off things as you accomplish them. On the list include schedules for the following.

- All the preliminary work that needs to be done, such as early shopping, making games or decorations, house-cleaning, reserving the rental of various items you may need, or calling to make special food orders.
- Cooking that can be done in advance and how far in advance. Some things like breads and soups can be made weeks before and frozen. A cheese ball can be made one to two days in advance. In addition to planning the cooking that can be done in advance, write out the order of cooking on the day of the event. Be sure you haven't planned things that need to bake at different tempera-tures at the same time, or too many things for the refrigerator space available. One hint: if you find you are preparing for an open house type of party and are running short of refrigerator space, which is easy to do when you are planning to serve a variety of fruits and vegetable platters, use an ice chest or two to store items as they are prepared. You can cut and clean vegetables, place them in an ice chest in plastic bags and they will be kept adequately chilled until serving time over some ice in the bottom.
- Things that will need to be done the day of the party and when to do them, such as setting up the table(s), making

coffee, tossing the salad, thawing rolls, whatever. Add any little notes that are important to you such as "don't forget to light candles," or "remember to set butter out to soften thirty minutes before guests arrive and put the salt and pepper shakers out at the same time." "Remember to start hot water for Mary's tea." Tailor this list for *you*.

These lists, if prepared properly, will give you a pretty good idea of the amount of work you have to do. At this time, you can see what changes you might want to make. Perhaps you will decide to purchase dessert, or hire a teenager to help set up or clean up. It is much easier to make these decisions on paper ahead of time than to try and frantically alter plans the day of a party.

Hints On Food Serving

(1) For any party of more than eight, a buffet is a good idea. When setting up a buffet, make sure people can circulate freely around the food table. If it will be crowded, have several food stations set up, perhaps the main dish, bread and vegetables on one table, salad on another, and beverages on another.

(2) Especially for a buffet, but also for any meal, be sure the food is easy to eat. Have the meat cut into realistic pieces for either a casserole or individual serving pieces. Make salad items bite-sized so guests don't have to try to cut huge pieces of lettuce while balancing a plate on their knees.

(3) Be creative in your use of serving pieces. You can place hot bowls in baskets if they fit. They will be easier to handle and will look good. Remember, too, that casserole dishes can also be used for salads, and pottery is great for all kinds of food service.

A Selection of Parties and Appropriate Menus

Following is a list of various types of entertainment occasions. Suggestions are included for specific events, possible variations, miscellaneous hints and menu ideas. Though you can use the menus and other suggestions just as they are given, feel free to alter them, combine them, use parts of one for an inspiration, and parts of another for future planning.

NOTE: Menu items for which this book contains the recipe are marked with an asterisk (*).

The Open House Party

This is what I think of as an all purpose party. It usually takes place in the evening, and can extend from 7:00 p.m. until 10:00 p.m. or later. It can, however, also take place in the early or late afternoon. This sort of party is relatively unstructured. Usually the group has something in common, and they are all invited over primarily for food and conversation. The atmosphere is usually rather casual, though how this definition works out in practice varies tremendously with different age groups and parts of the country.

Plastic ware, paper plates and napkins are always appropriate for this type of a gathering. Be sure to have several trash containers scattered about so your guests can toss used plates and cups as the party progresses.

This event can accommodate numerous situations. It is often a once-a-year gathering for many families who develop their own traditions. For example, one family might always host a party like this after their adult Sunday School class goes Christmas caroling. Another might annually have a party to celebrate the Fourth of July. Another could have a School's Out (or Started) Party. Groups can put this sort of party on as a reception to honor someone, or as a group wedding or baby shower. Where we live in the mountains of Colorado, I want to make it a tradition to have an open house each year as the aspen trees turn golden.

As to activities, if it is for a reception or shower, you may want a time when you participate in activities such as those described in the "Make a Memory" section of chapter 5. Otherwise, conversation will probably take care of itself. This is the sort of gathering that is especially appropriate for costume parties.

For decorations, you can have anything from a simple centerpiece to elaborate decorations. You can make your garage a circus tent or your living room a fantasy in green and red for Christmas. You can use only a few flowers or have ribbons and balloons over everything—whatever you would like.

MENU #1

Corn chips with bean dip
* Vegetable Platters with
  Avocado Dip and
  *Guacamole Dip
* Cheddar Nut Cheese Roll

Assortment of crackers
* Chicken Wings West
* Hazelnut Brownies
* Crunchy Peanut Butter
  Cookies

If desired, a * Melon Platter can be added.

MENU #2

---

* Vegetable Platter
  with Shrimp Cream Vegetable
  Stuffing thinned to Vegetable
  Dip consistency
* Melon Platter
* Pickled Mushrooms

Assorted crackers
Popcorn
* Cheddar Olive Cheese Log
* Chicken Wings Oriental
* Jimmy's Crab Goodies

83

A good beverage for both menus would be a simple punch of cranberry juice and 7-Up.

Brunch

Brunch is one of my favorite ways to entertain. The food for it is easy to prepare, the setting relaxing, and somehow having people over in the middle of the day on the weekend seems special.

You can have a brunch after church instead of a heavy Sunday dinner, or after any morning Bible Study, or for whatever other excuse you want to have one. A brunch is a nice way to honor someone or to have a quiet good-bye party for a friend who is moving.

Brunches work well served buffet style. Place additional salt, pepper and butter for rolls near where people will be sitting. Set up a big pot of water, such as a large coffee maker, and have all the beverages arranged around it.

Brunches do not require extensive decorations. A bouquet of fresh flowers in the middle of the table is lovely, or if it takes place in the fall, dried flowers or autumn leaves are all that is necessary to set a festive mood.

BRUNCH MENU

---

* Tuna Supper Pie
* Curried Shrimp and Eggs
  served over rice
* Melon Platter or * Sunny Citrus
  Salad

Sausage or ham slices, if desired
Sweet roll assortment or
  * Banana Muffins and Pumpkin
  Raisin Muffins

For beverages: coffee and tea, both regular and decaffeinated, plus herb teas, juices, or a combination of half juice/half mineral water, hot chocolate, if desired.

Buffets and Potlucks

These are a great way to feed a group of people without a lot of work because everyone shares in the preparation of the food. In addition to the work being shared, it's fun to sample the way different people prepare foods.

Decorations and activity ideas are the same as for Open House parties.

Though I have never attended a potluck that I did not think was fantastic, many people worry about the food, whether or not there will be a proper selection, or if it will be all salads and all desserts. If you are concerned about this, there are several ways to prevent the problem. First of all you can assign people categories of food to bring. For example, last names beginning with A-D bring a salad, E-F bring bread, et cetera. Or, if you want to be a bit more organized, you can do what one Sunday School class of over a hundred members did at a recent Christmas dinner they planned. A hospitality committee planned the menu and then copied the recipes for each item. Families in the class chose a copy of the recipe they wanted to make. The menu was very similar to Menu #1 below and the event turned out very well.

Another buffet/potluck idea is any sort of "build your own" set-up. This could be a salad bar, or a make-your-own-sandwich set-up. Either of these can be combined with a make-your-own ice-cream-sundae set-up for dessert. These are great, because nobody has to cook for them and people enjoy the fun of them. Whoever hosts the event provides paper plates or bowls, cups, knives, forks, napkins and the beverage. Guests can be assigned to bring the various food items for the buffet. For example:

Salad Bar Buffet

Cleaned and cut lettuce
Cleaned and cut spinach or variety lettuce
Sprouts
Shredded carrots
Chopped celery
Marinated green beans or other vegetables
Grated cheese
Chopped hard boiled eggs
Canned kidney or garbanzo beans
Various items such as artichoke hearts, mushrooms, etc.
Variety of salad dressings
Selection of hard rolls or sweet breads
Butter or margarine

Sandwich Buffet

A variety of sliced meats: ham, turkey, salami, etc.
A variety of sliced cheeses: swiss, cheddar, jack, etc.
A bowl of tuna salad
A bowl of egg salad
A platter of lettuce leaves
A platter of sliced tomatoes
A platter of sliced pickles
Different kinds of dark and light bread
Mustard, mayonnaise, horseradish spread
A couple of big bags of potato chips

Ice Cream Sundae Buffet

Just three kinds of ice cream: chocolate, vanilla and strawberry
A variety of toppings: fudge, butterscotch, marshmallow, caramel, etc.
Whipped cream, canned or of the Cool Whip variety
Maraschino cherries
Bananas or other chopped fruit
Chopped nuts
An assortment of small cookies

To decide who brings what, write the various items on slips of paper. Place them in a container and have everyone draw one out.

For the more standard buffet try the menus below.

MENU #1

---

* Chicken With Tomatoes   * Green Beans With Basil
* Marinated Mushroom Salad   * Company Sweet Rolls
Buttered pasta noodles   * Cherry Mincemeat Pie

MENU #2

---

* Guacamole Salad   * Spanish Macaroni
* Oven Green Chili   * Special Ice Creams
Buttered flour tortillas

Luncheons: Mens and Ladies

There are numerous reasons for entertaining at lunch, but more than many other kinds of entertaining, lunch time events seem to be those with a purpose other than fellowship. Often luncheon entertainment involves a speaker. This can be for the purpose of learning a skill such as how to be a better speaker, a seamstress or a teacher. It can be a fund raising event, perhaps with a slide show of a local ministry, or a country and missionary. Luncheons are often a time when business people can invite their co-workers to hear an evangelistic or inspirational message.

With the busy schedules everyone seems to have today, luncheons are best if they have easy to prepare, easy to eat, simple foods. The food should be satisfying, but not too heavy so that work can still be done throughout the remainder of the day. What this means depends, in large measure, on the group you are entertaining. Some groups would feel cheated if they did not have a full meal complete with meat, salad, vegetable, bread and dessert. Other groups would prefer a more simple soup and salad type of meal. Know your group and design the menu with them in mind.

The menus described for the Buffet/Potluck section can be used if a more complete, heavier meal is desired. But for a lighter soup and salad meal, try some of these suggestions.

MENU #1

* Tuna Potato Soup
* Cheesy Bran Muffins or
  * Oatmeal Honey Bread

* Green Bean Mushroom Salad
* Applesauce Cake With Lemon
  Sauce

MENU #2

* Chilled Fruit Soup
* Almond Shrimp Salad

* Company Sweet Rolls
* Sugarless Fruit Pie

MENU #3

* Salmon Cream Soup
* Soy Shrimp Salad

* Whole Wheat French Rolls
* Hazelnut Brownies

Dinner Parties

A dinner party is a great way to entertain people. You can talk through the entire meal and get to know the people better. It generally works best with eight people or less. If you have more, a buffet is usually a better choice.

The setting can be casual or formal. In most instances, no planned activity other than conversation is needed.

HOLIDAY DINNER #1

* Best Ever Turkey or
  * Barbecued Turkey
    Hindquarter
* Apple Sausage Stuffing or
  * Nutty Stuffing
* Sugar Free Cranberry Salad

* Maple Whipped Sweet
  Potatoes
* Steamed Broccoli With Basil
  Butter
* Pumpkin Raisin Muffins
* Velvet Pumpkin Cheesecake

HOLIDAY DINNER #2

* Orange Glazed Cornish Game
  Hens or * Lemon Roasted
  Game Hens
* Orange Wild Rice Stuffing
* Pomegranate Fruit Salad

* Steamed Broccoli With Basil
  Butter
* Company Sweet Rolls
* Cherry Mincemeat Pie

DINNER MENU #1

* Spinach Lasagna or * Spinach
  Manicotti or * Spaghetti Ala
  Carbonara

* Whole Wheat French Bread
  Tossed salad
  Ice cream and cookies

DINNER MENU #2

* Broccoli Cheese Chicken
* Poppy Seed Noodles
  Tossed salad

* Whole Wheat French Rolls
* Applesauce Bundt Cake With
  Lemon Sauce

After the Event Parties

Christmas caroling, a concert or play, even Sunday evening church—often after events such as these it is enjoyable to invite a group of people over to share a meal. Decorations really aren't necessary, and the food should be something that can be prepared ahead of time and is easy to serve. The menus below meet these requirements. Both main dishes can be assembled and put in the oven to be taken out as soon as you walk in the door.

These kinds of meals work well served buffet style. Have the buffet table completely ready, perhaps with a nice centerpiece. Have your serving pieces ready and as people arrive, set the food out on the table.

If you have a fireplace, and the weather is right, this is a pleasant time to enjoy it. Lay the fire before you leave, and when you return, you just have to light it.

MENU #1
---

* Oven Green Chili   Ice cream
* Jicama Pineapple Slaw   * Hazelnut Brownies
Buttered floured tortillas

MENU #2
---

* Oven Barley Beef   Hot apple cider
* Red Cabbage Slaw   Doughnuts
* Cheesy Bran Muffins

Afternoon Tea

A tea is a delightful way to spend an afternoon with

friends. You can use it for a baby shower, a wedding shower or to celebrate a birthday.

A tea works nicely if the guest list is not too large, six to eight people is a good number. Flowers and linens are the best decorations. You may have, or want to borrow, a silver tea service but a china tea set works very well also.

The "make a memory" suggestion in chapter 5 is a good activity, especially if the group consists of close friends.

MENU #1	MENU #2
Small sandwiches	An assortment of sweet breads
* Hazelnut Brownies	* Banana Muffins
* Lemon Snowballs	* Melon Platter

The beverage, of course, is tea, regular and herb, with sugar and cream.

Cookie Exchange

These events are especially fun during the holiday season. Each person brings several batches of whatever goodie they choose to make and then exchanges them with others in the group. The idea is that everyone gets to try the special treats everyone else makes, plus they get to take some new goodies home. You can either have everyone pre-package their goodies or you can combine the extras and split them up at the party.

If you wish, you can ask your guests to write out the recipes ahead of time and bring copies to give to each guest at the party.

Items That Could Be Used:
* Carob Cashew Cookies
* Lemon Snowballs
* Crunchy Peanut Butter Cookies
* Hazelnut Brownies
* Banana Muffins

Outdoor Meals or Picnics

The out-of-doors provides all the decorations you need for this event. The activities can be anything from a hike to a game of softball or soccer. The most important consideration is that the food travel well and be tasty at a variety of temperatures. In addition to some of the standard picnic fare of hot dogs and sandwiches, try some of the foods below for a delightful change.

MENU #1	MENU #2

* Cheddar Nut Cheese Log or
  * Cheese Platter
* Melon Platter or Assorted fruits
* Whole Wheat French Bread
* Hazelnut Brownies
* Carob Cashew Cookies
	* Chicken Wings Western or
	  * Lemon Roasted Game Hens
	* Peppers In Peppers Slaw
	* Whole Wheat French Rolls
	* Crunchy Peanut Butter Cookies
	* Lemon Snowballs

Portable Foods or Meals

These recipes are for the occasions when you are asked to contribute to a potluck, or if you want to take food to someone who has been ill or who, for some other reason, isn't able to cook at the present time. This kind of caring hospitality is usually greatly appreciated.

Foods That Travel Well: * Orange Rice Salad
                            * Broccoli and Beans Salad
                            * Frozen Vegetable Salad
                            * Tuna Supper Pie
                            * Lemon Rosemary Chicken
                            * Chicken Wings Western
                            * Whole Wheat French Bread
                            * Banana Muffins
                            * Any Of the Cookie Recipes

THE FOOD ITSELF

The previous chapter described a variety of parties with suggested menus. Following this chapter will be actual recipes for all sorts of hospitality events from specifically large group occasions to any occasion you desire. But this chapter will help you with the associated information you need when planning for various occasions. There will be notes on menu planning in general, ideas for foods to make ahead, how to plan quantities for a group, and finally, one of my favorite topics, how to garnish and present foods.

Menu Planning In General

When you plan a menu, keep the following guidelines in mind:

(1) First of all, tailor the menu to the mood of the party. If it is formal, don't serve pizza. If it's informal, don't serve Steak Diane. As obvious as this might seem, it is amazing how often this simple rule is broken. People think they have to make very exotic foods whenever they entertain. We can never be reminded enough to focus our minds on the people we are entertaining, not the preparation. When we remember that their comfort is the most important item on the schedule, the food planning becomes a relaxed, simple effort.

(2) Don't feel you have to make every menu item yourself. Many women who work want to entertain, but don't have the time to make every item from appetizers to desserts. If time is a problem, plan on making perhaps three items out of the five or six you will serve. For example, you can make the chicken casserole, tossed salad and a vegetable, but then purchase nice crackers and cheese for an appetizer, French bread to accompany the meal, and a bakery-made chocolate pie for dessert.

The purchase of even one or two items can greatly ease entertainment trauma. Become familiar with specialty shops and bakeries in your area so you know what you can count on from them. Then develop your own specialties and make your meals a cooperative success.

(3) One easy rule to remember in overall meal planning is that if you serve a simple meal (for example: homemade soup, tossed salad and crusty French bread), serve a fantastic dessert—like chocolate cheesecake or homemade apple pie with ice cream. If, on the other hand, you make a complex, heavy dinner such as lasagna with all the trimmings, a simple dessert such as lemon ice cream would be appropriate.

(4) In addition to deciding which foods to purchase and which foods to prepare yourself, determine which foods you can prepare ahead of time. For example, you can make many soups ahead and freeze them, as you can homemade breads or rolls. Many of the salads and main dish items in the recipe section can either be made a day ahead or assembled early on the day of the event. The important principle is to make certain you don't have more than one item, if that, which needs last minute attention. Getting a meal on the table after everything is prepared is difficult enough without having to worry about last minute, difficult foods.

(5) When menu planning, it helps to have a general idea of quantities in mind. In addition to general guidelines which will be given below, keep in mind the time of day and the meal being served. People usually plan to eat more at dinner than at lunch. An evening party or open house that takes place from 7:00 p.m. to 10:00 p.m. will require less food than one that takes place from 3:00 p.m. to 7:00 p.m. because most people will be hungry for dinner at the late afternoon party. It's also true that women tend to eat less than men, teenagers consume unbelievably large amounts of food and so do athletes. Keep these things in mind as you plan your menus and don't forget your own personal knowledge of your group. If you are cooking for a youth group and know most of the kids aren't crazy about salad, but love your homemade muffins, plan accordingly no matter what the charts say.

Some General Quantity Guidelines

(1) For an appetizer party, plan on serving 3-4 pieces per person on a total of 5-7 items. Plus, there should be at least one food item of unlimited quantity such as popcorn or chips and dip. The more items you have, the less you can plan on serving per item.

(2) When planning ice for beverages, figure about one pound of ice per person.

(3) For a buffet dinner, plan on 3-4 ounces of cooked fish or boneless meat per person or about 5-6 ounces uncooked. If the meat is bone-in, such as chicken or ribs, increase the amount by several ounces per person.

(4) For buffet servings of salads, potatoes and vegetable side dishes, count on about 2 cups per person total for all of the items combined. Another way to do it, if you are serving a

tossed salad, potato and vegetable item, is to plan on about 1 cup of tossed salad per person and 1 cup of potato or vegetable combined per person.

(5) Depending upon the group, figure 1-2 bread items per person.

Since it can't be stressed enough how different groups vary in their consumption of foods, get in the habit of making notes after each party. Note which foods were eaten quickly; what foods, if any, were depleted too soon; what equipment was used and how well it worked; what foods were easy or difficult to prepare and why.

Food Garnishing

The most simple foods in the world become special with a bit of garnishing. A plain fruit salad sprinkled with pomegranate seeds, a simple tossed salad with fresh nasturtium flowers, a cream pie with chocolate curls on top— little things really do mean a lot when it comes to food. In addition to the garnishing done to the food itself, there are a number of ways to serve food that are a garnish in themselves. These include using baskets and wooden cutting boards as serving pieces.

The wonderful variety of ways to garnish food is almost endless. This section will give a variety of ideas to get you started, but always keep your eyes open. When you see an idea in a magazine, cut it out or note it down and put it in your hostess notebook. When you see an attractive idea at a restaurant or buffet, note it also and try your own variation of it later. Envision these ideas:

(1) Parsley is an old, tried and true food garnish and it is wonderful. To keep it fresh when you bring it home, wash it,

cut off the bottoms and then set it in a container of water in the refrigerator until you are ready to use it.

There are numerous other greens that can also be used to line vegetable and fruit platters and to form the base for other foods. For example, consider some of the various kinds of greens and lettuce. Endive is an interesting accent as are mustard greens, collard and other sorts of greens. If you grow chard in your garden, it makes a lovely platter liner, especially if you have the variety with the ruby colored stalks.

(2) Color coordinating with your food garnishes always looks nice. The easiest time to do this is at Christmas when you can work into your Christmas meals: red peppers, cranberries, cherry tomatoes, radishes and red apples. Combine some of these with green peppers, broccoli florets, snap peas, cucumbers, spinach and green apples.

Some specific ways to combine these are to decorate your table with a wreath made with leaf spinach and cherry tomatoes or cranberries. You can also cover a styrofoam tree with parsley and then place cheese cubes on toothpicks on it.

(3) In the spring use your colored Easter eggs as a centerpiece.

(4) You can combine vegetables for visual interest. For example, peel and slice a red onion into rings about ½ - 1 inch thick. Cut carrot or celery sticks and place them into the onion rings and you have an attractive red tie around the vegetables.

(5) Many varieties of fruits and vegetables can be used as attractive containers for other foods. Green and red peppers, cucumber and zucchini boats all are great for cold salads and similar foods. Melons and pineapples are, of course, wonderful for fruit salads, but don't forget orange or lemon

baskets for desserts, sherbets and small amounts of foods.

In the winter, a large pumpkin or hollowed out squash makes a great container for soup. Cabbages, both green and red, can be hollowed out as containers for salad or vegetable dips.

(6) To present sliced meats attractively, roll them or fold them. Sprinkle sliced olives on top for a garnish. If you are serving sliced cheese at the same time, you can roll it also and alternate it with the rolled meat around the platter.

(7) Any food put on skewers looks special. You can find the small bamboo skewers at specialty food shops. Try putting a selection of fruit on them such as chunks of melon, pineapple and strawberries. Or skewer pieces of meat and cheese, or combine meat such as ham with pineapple slices, or cold beef with small cherry tomatoes and small pickles.

(8) When making sandwiches, use one whole wheat and one white slice of bread. Cut the sandwich into three long strips and remove the outer crusts. Suddenly a simple sandwich becomes more special than if made with just white bread and cut in half.

(9) Small fruits such as grapes and strawberries can be dipped into a beaten egg white and then into sugar to garnish all sorts of dishes. A ham or fish looks lovely with green grapes, a fruit dessert becomes elegant with sugared strawberries.

(10) Keep on hand some commercial food garnishes. For example, colored sugar sprinkles are simple and fun to use. On the more exotic side, candied violets and rose petals can be used to top any frosted dessert or one topped with whipped cream. These lovely items make the simplest foods quite elegant.

(11) Layering foods in clear glass serving pieces also makes

any item look special. For example, layer canned and drained vegetables in a glass bowl, top with dressing, and toss just before serving.

(12) Don't forget garnishes for soup: croutons, a dollop of sour cream or plain yogurt touches up even a simple tomato soup.

(13) Rice easily becomes an elegant side dish when it is molded in a ring. Just pack hot cooked rice into a generously buttered ring mold. Unmold at once by placing a serving dish on top and inverting. If desired, place vegetables inside the ring.

(14) To have perfect hard-cooked eggs for appetizers or as slices for garnishes, use eggs that are several days old.

(15) Even butter becomes decorative when you make butter curls. Dip the butter curler into lukewarm water and then pull it firmly across chilled butter. Refrigerate the pieces until serving time. You can make chocolate curls the same way by using the butter curler over a bar of chocolate.

(16) One final note, never use as a garnish anything that cannot be eaten such as plastic figures, ivy leaves, or non-edible flowers. This is particularly true for an event attended by children.

10
ENTERTAINING A LARGE GROUP

Food and sharing, talking and eating, so much of the time we spend together seems to revolve around food—and it is a wonderful way to spend time with those you care about. Besides, eating together is fun. Maybe it's a couple's church banquet, a missionary supper, a dinner for new members, a youth group meal, or any of the multitude of activities that come up in the life of a church or any large group of people.

Essential as these activities are, and as much enjoyment as you know will come from them, few cause the people involved more fear and panic than being responsible to feed lots of people. If this should happen to you, remember you aren't the first to feel that feeding a large group was impossible.

"Give them something to eat."
Can you imagine the disciples' concern when Jesus said that?

There they were on a hot, Palestinian hillside surrounded by 5,000 hungry people. Probably out of frustration, one of the disciples reminded Jesus that they only had five loaves and two fish.

"Bring them to me," Jesus said.

Out of that seemingly inadequate beginning, in the hands of Jesus, there became enough for everyone.

(Matthew 14:16-20)

"Bring them to me." The solution is still the same. Though this chapter will give you tips, recipes and menus, any meal prepared for a Christian group is of vital concern to our Lord. We are feeding His people, in His name and He is Guest of Honor. It is safe to assume He is also vitally concerned with all aspects of the food preparation.

Over the years I have cooked for groups of 20-500 and it's never easy. I'm constantly praying, "Lord, give me wisdom on menu planning," "Please stretch the meat to feed all those hungry kids." "Lord, please let the ovens be working this time and help me to squeeze all the things I need into the refrigerator." And I know He has promised to care for all of the little things in life—and that includes cooking for crowds.

Menu Planning

Below are some planned menu suggestions to help you get started. In general, when you plan your own menus, keep the following suggestions in mind:

(1) Prepare main dishes that taste good at almost any serving temperature. It's hard to have food really hot when you cook for most groups unless you have steam tables. Chicken, for example, tastes good at almost any temperature. Prime rib and many other cuts of beef don't. Hamburger casseroles, however, retain their flavor as they cool.

(2) Always plan simple desserts like cakes and pies that need no last minute preparation. Simple bowls of ice cream

are also fine for casual meals.

(3) If you have made most of the meal from scratch and oven space is limited, buy your bread product. If you want a homemade product, make your bread ahead and freeze it.

All of the recipes below are for 24. They can be easily made in multiples to serve several hundred. When you multiply a recipe, though, never use a strict multiplication of the spices. For instance, if the multiple of three times the garlic powder required in a recipe would be 1½ teaspoons, a little less than one teaspoon would probably be all right. Always use a little less seasoning to begin with, taste and adjust from there. Also, when you increase a recipe, for some reason it makes more than if you just multiplied the number of servings. For example, many hamburger casseroles that would serve six, if you multiply the recipe by three, will probably serve 20-22 instead of 18.

When planning amounts, remember there is no exact method. As we've already said, men and teenagers do eat more than most women. People tend to eat more at dinner than at lunch. To ensure that your main dish goes far enough, never place it first in a buffet line. Place your salad first, then bread and vegetables, and the meat or main dish last. With less space left on their plates, people will take less than they would if they meet the yummy main dish casserole with a completely empty plate.

Equipment Planning

When cooking for a large crowd, you need to be certain you have the right equipment.

Begin by checking out your oven. Many church and

institutional ovens are not at all accurate. Ask someone who has used them before and never cook something that is delicate, like meringues, in them. Also, be careful not to plan your baking times too closely with these ovens. If something needs to cook for 1½ hours, plan to have it done at least ½ an hour before it has to be served. That way, if the oven is cooking slow, you have some extra time to make sure it gets done, and if it is done, you can just turn the oven to warm.

Be sure you have enough serving and baking dishes. Borrow or rent them if you don't. Though stainless steel steam table pans are ideal to cook large quantities in, they are very expensive. A good substitute are 9" x 13" regular baking pans. They will hold about 12 servings of a main dish, and they fit well into ovens.

Check out the refrigerator both in terms of space available and who else may be using it. I was once told I could use some refrigerator space at church, but the day of the planned dinner it was filled with milk for a children's church outing. Even if you know you can use the whole refrigerator, plan your use of the space carefully.

People Planning

When planning a group cooking event, be sure you have enough people to help. You will need people to help set-up, people to help cook, and if at all possible, a separate group to clean up.

Sample Menus

The following menus are for a variety of occasions and use the recipes given below. Feel free to change dishes or to modify them if you have other favorite recipes.

FANCY DINNER MENU

This is the kind of menu that is nice for a special group or church dinner such as a Valentine's banquet, missionary fund raiser, or that sort of thing. Though this menu can be served buffet style, it works nicely for a sit-down dinner also.

Lemon Herb Baked Chicken
Seasoned Carrots and Zucchini
Two-Toned Tossed Salad With Western French Dressing
Sweet Bran Muffins
Chocolate Peanut Butter Pie

SOUP SUPPER MENU

This inexpensive, easy meal works well for anything from a small luncheon to a large fund raising dinner. I used a similar menu once for a fund raiser at which we fed around 300 people.

Hamburger Stew   Corn Oatmeal Muffins
Easy Slaw   Small bowls of ice cream

CASUAL/KIDS SUPPER MENU

This is a great meal for teen or college age people. It's hearty, tasty and healthy.

Sloppy Josès
Sunny Citrus Salad
Extra corn chips or Peanut Butter Bran Muffins
Honey Orange Snacking Cake

RECIPES

LEMON HERB BAKED CHICKEN

When you cut up chickens for serving to a crowd, cut each breast into 3 pieces lengthwise, instead of in half. If the thighs are large, cut them in half. By doing this you get more pieces of equal size. In addition, you should always skin your chicken. This removes the fat, making it more healthful, and chicken tastes better baked when it is skinned.

6 chickens, cut up and skinned	1 t. garlic powder
4 onions, sliced	1 t. rosemary
2 lemons, sliced	½ t. marjoram
1 c. lemon juice	dash pepper
1 t. salt	paprika

Use two 9" x 13" baking pans. Place half of the chicken in each pan. Put the onion and lemon slices on top of the chicken. Combine the lemon juice, salt, garlic powder, rosemary, marjoram, and pepper and sprinkle over the chicken. Cover pan tightly with foil and bake at 350° for about 90 minutes. Baste a couple of times to keep chicken moist. Just before serving, sprinkle with paprika for garnish. Serves 24.

HAMBURGER STEW

2 lb. ground beef	16 oz. tomato sauce
2 large onions, chopped	10-12 c. water
32 oz. frozen, mixed vegetables	2 T. Worchestershire sauce
32 oz. tomatoes, chopped and undrained	2 t. garlic salt
5 potatoes, cubed	1 t. pepper

continued on next page

Hamburger Stew, continued

Place the ground beef and chopped onions in a large soup pot. Cook over medium heat until ground beef is well browned. Drain off grease. Add remaining ingredients; bring to a boil and simmer 45 minutes. Adjust seasonings to taste and if needed, add additional water. Serves 24.

SLOPPY JOSE'S

Similar to Sloppy Joes, but these have a tangy south-of-the-border flavor. An additional plus when serving these for a large group is that they are a complete main dish served out of the pan. There is no need for a bun.

2 lb. ground beef	1 t. salt
2 c. onions, diced	1 T. chili powder
6 c. pinto beans, cooked (use either canned or home cooked)	1 t. garlic powder
	1 t. cumin
6 c. canned tomatoes pureed with the juice	½ of a 16 oz. package of corn chips
1 c. tomato paste	1 c. grated cheddar cheese
1 small can green chili peppers	1 16 oz. jar salsa—optional

NOTE: You can use more or less of the green chili peppers depending on how spicy you want the final product.

Brown the ground beef and onions in a large skillet or kettle on top of the stove. Drain grease and divide the mixture into two 9" x 13" baking pans. In the same skillet stir together the pinto beans, tomatoes, tomato paste, chili peppers, salt, chili powder, garlic powder and cumin. Divide this mixture equally into the pans with the browned ground beef and stir to combine. Cover with foil and place in 350° oven for about 1 hour. Just before serving, remove foil and sprinkle corn chips on top. Sprinkle grated cheddar cheese on top and return to oven for 5-10 minutes or until cheese melts. Serve with additional salsa on the side if desired. Serves 24.

SEASONED CARROTS AND ZUCCHINI

4 lb. fresh carrots
4 lb. fresh zucchini
⅔ c. melted butter

2 t. marjoram
1 t. seasoned salt

In separate, large kettles steam the carrots and the zucchini until each is just tender. (This needs to be done separately because the carrots take longer to cook than the zucchini.) When both are tender, combine in one pot and add the melted butter, marjoram and seasoned salt. Stir gently to coat the vegetables with the butter, marjoram and seasoned salt. Divide the vegetables in half and place in two baking dishes. Cook in 350° oven for about 15 minutes. Serves 24.

TWO-TONED TOSSED SALAD

The ingredients below can be varied tremendously according to personal taste and what happens to be available at various times during the year.

¼ c. green onions, chopped
3 cucumbers, sliced
4 carrots, grated
1 bunch radishes, sliced

4 tomatoes, cubed
1 head iceburg lettuce
3 heads leaf lettuce
1 c. dressing, see below

In the bottom of a very large bowl place the green onions, cucumbers, carrots, radishes and tomatoes. Pour the dressing over the vegetables. Tear the iceburg lettuce into chunks and place it on top. Next, tear the leaf lettuce into chunks and place it on top. Cover lettuce with plastic wrap and place in refrigerator until needed. Toss the salad just before serving.

Note: the easiest way to toss this salad is with your hands. Serves 24.

WESTERN FRENCH DRESSING

This is a sweet, tangy dressing everybody loves. It is much better to make one dressing and toss the salad with it than to have everyone add their own. By tossing the salad ahead of time, it costs less, and is much neater and faster in the serving line.

½ c. sugar	1 t. dried celery seed
¼ c. cider vinegar	1 t. salt
½ c. salad oil	1 t. paprika
½ c. catsup	1 T. finely grated onion

In a pint jar, stir together the sugar and cider vinegar until the sugar is dissolved. Add remaining ingredients and blend well. You may use a blender or food processor if you have one. Makes enough to toss a salad for 24.

SUNNY CITRUS SALAD

This can be made several hours ahead and kept refrigerated until ready to eat. The bananas won't turn dark because of the lime and orange juice in the salad.

15 bananas, sliced	12 oranges, peeled and cut into
3 20 oz. cans pineapple chunks,	chunks
drained but with the juice	½ c. lime juice
reserved	¼ c. honey or sugar

Combine the fruit in a large bowl. In another bowl combine the reserved pineapple juice, lime juice and honey or sugar to make a dressing. Stir until honey or sugar is dissolved. Toss fruit with the dressing. Serves 24.

EASY SLAW

2 heads cabbage, shredded	⅓ c. honey or sugar
2 green peppers, shredded	2 T. salt
1 red pepper, shredded	1 t. white pepper
⅔ c. cider vinegar	1 t. celery seed
⅔ c. vegetable oil	

Place shredded cabbage and peppers in a large bowl. In another bowl combine remaining ingredients, stirring until honey (or sugar) and salt are dissolved. Toss cabbage and peppers with this dressing. Serves 24.

HONEY ORANGE SNACKING CAKE

¾ c. butter or margarine, softened	1½ t. baking soda
¾ c. honey or brown sugar	½ t. salt
3 eggs	1 orange, pureed in a blender or food processor
1 t. orange extract	
½ c. orange juice	¾ c. raisins
3 c. whole wheat pastry flour or unbleached flour	¾ c. chopped walnuts

In a medium sized bowl, beat together the butter or margarine and the honey or brown sugar. Add the eggs one by one and beat well after each. Beat in the orange extract and orange juice. In another bowl, stir together the flour, baking soda and salt. Add this to the other mixture and combine well. Stir in pureed orange, raisins and walnuts. Bake in a greased and floured 9" x 13" pan for 35-45 minutes at 350° or until a toothpick inserted in the center comes out clean. Serves 24.

CORN OATMEAL MUFFINS

2 c. unbleached flour
1 c. corn meal
1 c. oatmeal
2 t. baking powder
1½ t. salt

1 t. baking soda
2 c. buttermilk
2 eggs
1 c. butter or margarine, melted
⅔ c. honey or brown sugar

Grease well 24 muffin cups. In one bowl stir together the flour, corn meal, oatmeal, baking powder, salt and baking soda. In another bowl combine the buttermilk, eggs, melted butter or margarine, and honey or brown sugar. Combine the two mixtures, stirring until just mixed. Spoon into muffin cups and bake at 400° for 15-20 minutes or until lightly browned. Makes 24.

CHOCOLATE PEANUT BUTTER PIE

This is so rich and good—it's a little like eating a giant Reese's Peanut Butter Cup.

4 prepared chocolate crumb pie crusts, or plain baked pie crusts
4 8 oz. packages cream cheese, softened
4 c. peanut butter

4 c. honey
2 c. whipping cream
1 T. vanilla extract
1 c. chocolate chips or chopped peanuts for garnish

Set the pie crusts out ready to be filled. In a large mixing bowl cream together the peanut butter and cream cheese. Add the honey and beat well. In another bowl, beat the whipping cream until stiff; add and beat in the vanilla. Fold peanut butter mixture into the whipped cream. Spoon mixture into pie shells. Sprinkle chocolate chips or chopped peanuts on top. Chill until serving time. Serves 24.

PEANUT BUTTER BRAN MUFFINS

2¼ c. whole wheat or unbleached flour
4 t. baking powder
1 t. salt
½ t. baking soda
2 eggs, beaten

2 c. milk
½ c. vegetable oil
2 c. bran cereal
⅔ c. chunky peanut butter
1 c. honey

Grease 24 muffin cups well. In one bowl combine the eggs, milk, oil and bran cereal. Let this mixture stand 5 minutes. In another bowl stir together the flour, baking powder, salt and baking soda. Add the peanut butter and honey to the liquid mixture and combine. Stir in dry mixture until just moistened. Spoon into muffin cups and bake at 400° about 15-20 minutes or until lightly browned. Makes 24.

SWEET BRAN MUFFINS

2 c. whole wheat flour
2 c. bran cereal
5 t. baking powder
1 t. salt

½ c. cooking oil
¾ c. honey or brown sugar
2 eggs
1¼ c. milk

In one bowl mix together the flour, bran cereal, baking powder and salt. In another bowl stir together the cooking oil, honey or brown sugar, eggs and milk. Combine the two mixtures, stirring just until lumpy. Fill well greased muffin cups ⅓ full. Bake at 400° for 10-15 minutes or until lightly browned. Makes 24.

11
RECIPES

. . . God loves a cheerful giver. And God is able to make all grace abound to you, so that in all things at all times, having all that you need, you will abound in every good work. As it is written: "He has scattered abroad his gifts to the poor; his righteousness endures for ever." Now he who supplies seed to the sower and bread for food will also supply and increase your store of seed and will enlarge the harvest way so that you can be generous on every occasion, and through us your generosity will result in thanksgiving to God.

II Corinthians 9:7b-11

APPETIZERS

Appetizers are one of the most useful and versatile of party foods. You can create a complete party menu from a variety of them. They are the wonderful components of late night snacks or the basis for any impromptu gathering. Appetizers are especially necessary before a dinner party—they give the hostess time to put the finishing touches on the main meal.

With appetizers, the visual appeal of the food is very important. Try to arrange foods in a design on a platter or coordinate food items by color. For example, make one vegetable platter all green and white by using green onions, broccoli, cauliflower, jicama and mushrooms. Another platter could be red and green by using celery, green onions, cherry tomatoes and radishes. Edible fresh flowers, vegetable garnishes, parsley, etc., can be used to liven up any appetizer. See the section on Food Garnishing in chapter 9 for a complete discussion of the subject.

Be brave and have fun with appetizers. You can always serve some simple ones like vegetable platters and chips. But you can also indulge in small amounts of expensive or exotic foods such as expensive cheeses, smoked oysters or mussels, caviar, shrimp and crab.

In addition to the small amounts of expensive appetizers, always have one or two "unlimited" items such as lots of crisp, raw vegetables, a large basket of flavorful crackers, or a big bowl of popcorn on hand.

VEGETABLE TRAYS

Appropriate for any occasion, fresh vegetables and tasty dips are always welcome. By their very nature they are healthful and refreshing, and a delightful change from many heartier appetizers. They are also a courteous consideration for those watching their weight.

To save time, you can clean and cut vegetables early the day of the party or the night before, placing them in a plastic container with a lid that seals well. You can also use some of the heavy duty plastic bags that have a tight seal. Add a little water and a few crushed ice cubes to keep the vegetables crisp, then store them in the refrigerator until you are ready to use them. They can be arranged on a serving platter an hour or so before the party. After arranging them, spray or sprinkle a few drops of water on the platter, cover it with plastic wrap or foil, and return it to the refrigerator. With this done, the moment your guests arrive, you'll have a lovely platter of goodies for them to enjoy while you finish the last-minute meal preparation details.

VEGETABLE DIPS AND STUFFINGS

The recipes below fall into two categories. The "Dips" are designed to be the standard product into which your guests can dip raw vegetables. "Stuffings" have two uses. They can be stuffed into raw vegetables such as celery sticks, cherry tomatoes or mushroom caps, thus making some unique, tasty and attractive appetizers. Or, they can also be made into vegetable dips by thinning them with milk, sour cream or yogurt. All the dips can be made a day ahead or early on the day they are to be served.

AVOCADO DIP

This is a delicately flavored and delicious dip not quite as spicy as the Guacamole recipe.

1 avocado, very soft & ripe
½ c. sour cream
dash salt

1-2 t. Rose's Lime Juice or fresh lime juice

Mash avocado with a fork in a medium sized bowl. Add other ingredients and combine well. Makes about 1½ cups.

FOOD PROCESSOR PROCEDURE: Place all ingredients in food processor using the metal blade and blend for about 1 minute.

EASIEST EVER GUACAMOLE

In addition to working well as a vegetable dip, this recipe is also delicious as a dip with corn or tortilla chips. It is good as a garnish over any sort of Mexican food, too.

1 avocado, soft and ripe
2 t. lemon juice
¼ c. red taco sauce or salsa
¼ t. salt

⅛ t. pepper
1 T. finely chopped green onion
dash Tabasco sauce, optional

Mash avocado well with a fork in a medium sized bowl. Add remaining ingredients and mix well. Season to taste with more salt and pepper. If desired, add Tabasco sauce. Makes about 1 cup.

FOOD PROCESSOR PROCEDURE: Place all ingredients in food processor. Using the metal blade, blend for about 1 minute.

STILTON SHRIMP AND CHEESE VEGETABLE STUFFING

Though you can substitute any mild bleu cheese for the Stilton cheese, the Stilton gives it a wonderful touch.

1 c. Stilton cheese, softened   dash salt and pepper
¼ c. canned shrimp, finely chopped   1 t. lemon juice

Combine all ingredients in a medium sized bowl. Makes about 1⅓ cups.

FOOD PROCESSOR PROCEDURE: Blend all ingredients in processor using metal blade for about 1 minute.

SHRIMP CREAM VEGETABLE STUFFING

Absolutely elegant in taste, this filling is especially nice for stuffing fresh mushrooms.

4 oz. cream cheese, softened   1 t. lemon juice
2 T. walnuts, finely chopped   pinch each of crushed dried tarra-
1 4 oz. can shrimp pieces   gon, dill weed, salt and pepper
2 T. fresh mushrooms, finely
  chopped

Combine all ingredients in a medium sized bowl. Makes about 1½ cups.

FOOD PROCESSOR PROCEDURE: Place metal blade in processor, add walnuts and mushrooms; chop briefly. Add other ingredients and combine well.

BLEU CHEESE VEGETABLE STUFFING

This hearty dip is popular with men.

⅓ c. bleu cheese, crumbled   1 T. pecans, finely chopped
¼ c. plain yogurt or sour cream   dash garlic salt

Combine all ingredients in a medium sized bowl. Makes about ¾ cup.

FOOD PROCESSOR PROCEDURE: Insert metal blade in processor; chop pecans. Add other ingredients and combine for about 1 minute.

HEATED MUSHROOM APPETIZERS

This is a tasty way to use any of the vegetable stuffings above.

12 fresh, clean mushroom caps, medium to large in size
½ - ¾ c. any vegetable stuffing, recipes above

Using a teaspoon, place a dab of the vegetable dip in each mushroom cap and put the filled caps in any ovenproof container. At this point they can be refrigerated for up to 4 hours. Fifteen minutes before serving, bake mushrooms in a preheated 350° oven until tender. They may also be heated in a microwave for about 5 minutes on high power. Makes 12.

CURRY VEGETABLE STUFFING

⅓ c. pecans, chopped
8 oz. cream cheese, softened
1 t. curry powder

1 8 oz. can crushed pineapple, drained

Combine all ingredients in a medium sized bowl. Makes about ¾ cup.

FOOD PROCESSOR PROCEDURE: Place metal blade in processor. Chop pecans; add other ingredients and blend for about 1 minute.

CHEESE BALLS, LOGS AND SPREADS

The recipes below are tremendously versatile. Once the basic mixture is made, it can be shaped into balls or logs or put into crocks or serving bowls. In addition to being good appetizers, the cheese balls, logs and filled crocks also make nice hostess gifts.

FOOD PROCESSOR NOTE: Cheese balls are very easy to make with a food processor, and the procedure is the same for all of them. Using the metal blade, first chop up whatever garnish the finished ball will be rolled in such as parsley or nuts. Set this chopped mixture aside. Then chop ingredients such as onions, nuts and olives if the recipe calls for them. Leaving these chopped products in the processor, add the cheese and other ingredients and blend well. There is no need to grate the cheese before adding it to the processor, but it is advisable to break it into several pieces.

BLEU CHEESE LOG

Hearty and filling, this is always a favorite at parties. Rye or whole wheat crackers are good with this strong tasting cheese log.

1 c. grated bleu, Gorgonzola or Stilton cheese
4 oz. cream cheese, softened
1 T. Worchestershire sauce
½ medium onion, minced very finely
1 t. garlic powder
½ c. fresh parsley, finely chopped

Combine all ingredients but parsley with a fork in a medium sized bowl. Form into the desired shape, either a log or ball. Roll in chopped, fresh parsley. Chill well. Serve with crackers. Makes 1 medium sized cheese ball.

CHEDDAR NUT CHEESE ROLL

If you don't know the taste preferences of your guests, this recipe always works well.

1 c. cheddar cheese, grated
½ c. butter or margarine, softened
4 oz. cream cheese, softened
¼ t. Tabasco sauce
1 t. chili powder
dash salt and pepper
½ c. chopped walnuts
a few whole walnuts for garnish
paprika

Using a fork, combine all ingredients except walnuts in a medium sized bowl. After forming into the desired shape, roll in chopped walnuts and garnish with whole walnuts. Sprinkle with paprika for additional garnish. Makes 1 medium cheese ball.

CHEDDAR OLIVE CHEESE BALL

1 c. cheddar cheese, grated
1 c. Monterey jack cheese, grated
4 oz. cream cheese, softened
1 4 oz. can black olives, pitted
  and chopped

½ c. walnuts, chopped
1 t. garlic powder
dash Worchestershire sauce
¼ t. salt
dash pepper

Thoroughly combine all ingredients with a fork in a medium sized bowl. Form into desired shape and chill. Serve with crackers. Makes one fairly large cheese ball.

CHEESE BOARDS

Not all appetizers require extensive preparation. Some of the most delicious appetizers, like selections of good cheese, are also some of the easiest to prepare.

3-4 oz. chunks of several cheeses such as bleu, brie, gouda, swiss, cheddar or numerous other, more exotic varieties
an assortment of crackers

About an hour before your guests arrive, set the cheeses out and allow them to come to room temperature. Place with or near them a platter of assorted crackers, and you have a party treat everyone enjoys.

HINTS:
(1) Be sure to select good quality cheeses. Do not use the "processed cheese foods." Try different flavors of cheese. If you are unsure of what kind to buy, there are many wonderful cheese shops that will give you excellent suggestions.
(2) Fresh fruits such as pieces of apples, pears, or a variety of grapes are delicious served with cheese.

PICKLED MUSHROOMS

These yummy little treats are a great way to use small, very fresh mushrooms. They are also a nice addition to a platter of fresh vegetables.

1 c. cider vinegar	2 cloves garlic, minced or pressed
1 c. water	¼ c. cider vinegar
1 T. pickling spices	1 t. salt
3 c. small, fresh mushrooms	1 t. pepper
¼ c. olive oil	

Combine 1 cup of the cider vinegar, the water, and the pickling spices in a medium saucepan. Bring to a boil and boil for 10 minutes. Strain out the loose spices and return the liquid to the saucepan. Add the fresh mushrooms and again bring to a boil. Reduce heat and cook gently for 5 minutes. Drain off liquid and place mushrooms in a medium sized bowl.

In small skillet, heat the olive oil and garlic together for about 3 minutes over low heat. Then pour oil and garlic over mushrooms. Add cider vinegar, salt and pepper. Allow to marinate overnight or up to 2 days. Drain and serve. Makes about 2 cups.

The leftover marinade makes a nice salad dressing, and any remaining mushrooms make a delicious addition to tossed salads.

CHICKEN WING APPETIZERS

Chicken wings work well as an appetizer for several reasons. First of all, they are very inexpensive; and you can serve a huge platter of them at a party without destroying your budget. Second, they can be assembled the night before and cooked any time the day of the party because they are good served at any temperature. Last, people enjoy them because they are a satisfying "real food," not just a taste-tempting tidbit.

When purchasing chicken wings, you can buy the whole ones, but many restaurants and discount food supply houses also sell chicken wings that are pre-cut and have the wing tip removed. A whole bag of these is quite inexpensive and easy to use. If you use them in the recipes below, just substitute 2 or 3 pieces for each whole chicken wing.

CHICKEN WINGS ORIENTAL

These chicken wings have a yummy teriyaki flavor. They are especially nice when served as part of an Oriental buffet. If you don't have time to make everything from scratch, serve these with some frozen egg rolls and other Oriental appetizers. Add a few fortune cookies and you've got a quick and easy Oriental theme buffet.

12-18 chicken wings
½ c. unsweetened pineapple juice
½ c. soy sauce
½ c. vegetable oil
1 t. ground ginger

1 T. honey or brown sugar
1 t. garlic powder
1 T. dehydrated onion flakes
½ t. curry powder

Place chicken wings in a 9" x 13" baking dish. Combine remaining ingredients in a medium bowl, and pour over chicken wings. Allow to marinate in refrigerator for at least 4 hours or overnight, turning once or twice. When ready to bake, heat oven to 350° and bake uncovered 30-45 minutes. Baste several times while baking, until all wings are well done. Serves 6-8.

CHICKEN WINGS WESTERN

12-18 chicken wings
1 6 oz. can tomato paste
½ medium onion, finely chopped
1 t. garlic powder
½ t. chili powder

¼ c. cider vinegar
2 T. Worcestershire sauce
⅓ c. honey or brown sugar
1 t. powdered mustard
dash salt and pepper

Place chicken wings in a 9" x 13" baking pan. Combine remaining ingredients in a medium bowl, and then pour mixture over the chicken wings. If they are not to be cooked immediately, cover pan with foil and refrigerate. To cook, heat oven to 350° and bake uncovered 30-45 minutes or until well done. Baste several times during the baking process. Serves 6-8.

JIMMY'S CRAB GOODIES

These taste fantastic and are perfect for a very special party or pre-dinner appetizer.

½ c. butter, softened
4 oz. cream cheese, softened
dash garlic powder
6 English muffins

1 4 oz. can crab meat, drained
and flaked
paprika for garnish

Combine butter, cream cheese, garlic powder and crab meat with a fork in a medium sized bowl. Halve muffins and spread crab mixture on them. Cut into quarters and place on a baking sheet. Sprinkle with a bit of paprika for garnish. Cover and keep frozen until ready to serve. At serving time, remove from freezer and place under preheated broiler until browned, about 3-5 minutes. Makes 4-6 servings.

BEVERAGES

The beverages served with any party or meal should be quite simple and inconspicuous. Nothing is worse than an overly sweet liquid one is forced to choke down. Serve either plain water, iced tea made with regular or herb tea, or milk during the meal, and offer regular or decaffeinated tea and/or coffee, during dessert.

For a party, one of the best and simplest punches is made with fruit juice combined with equal amounts of club soda or 7-Up. Orange juice or cranberry juice are very tasty and appropriate for any buffet, open house, reception or other gathering.

BREADS

The smell of homemade bread baking is a wonderful way to welcome guests. Homemade breads make the simplest of meals a special treat and help fill out any menu. The breads below are not difficult to make and all of them can be made ahead and frozen.

COMPANY SWEET ROLLS

These rolls are nice for a fancy dinner or for a ladies' luncheon.

2 pkg. or 2 T. active dry yeast	2 t. salt
¼ t. sugar	3 eggs
½ c. lukewarm water	¼ c. powdered milk
1¼ c. water	1 t. lemon rind
¾ c. honey or sugar	2 c. whole wheat flour
½ c. oil	5-6 c. unbleached flour
½ c. butter or margarine	

Dissolve yeast in ½ cup lukewarm water in a small bowl. In a large bowl combine 1¼ cups water, honey, oil, butter or margarine, eggs, powdered milk and lemon rind. Stir until honey or sugar and salt are dissolved. Add whole wheat flour and then stir in unbleached flour until a stiff dough forms. Knead for 5-10 minutes or until dough is smooth and elastic. Place in a lightly greased bowl and cover with a cloth. Allow to rise at room temperature until doubled in bulk.

Punch down and form dough into rolls of any shape. Place on greased cookie sheets, cover with cloths, and allow to rise until they again double in bulk, about ½ hour. Then bake in a preheated 400° oven for 15-20 minutes, or until lightly browned. Makes about 4 dozen rolls.

WHOLE WHEAT FRENCH BREAD

Made in the traditional shape or as rolls, this crunchy bread is a treat that goes with any meal.

1 pkg. or 1 T. active dry yeast	¾ c. reconstituted powdered milk
½ t. sugar	2 t. salt
¼ c. lukewarm water	¾ c. water
2 T. melted butter or margarine	4-5 c. whole wheat flour
¼ c. sugar or honey	

Dissolve sugar in ¼ cup water and then dissolve yeast in this. Set it aside for about 5 minutes. In a large bowl combine the melted butter or honey, milk, salt and water. Stir until the salt and honey or sugar are dissolved. Stir in yeast mixture. Add flour one cup at a time and stir. Add enough flour until a fairly stiff dough is formed. Turn dough out of the bowl and knead for about 10 minutes. Place dough back into a large, clean, lightly greased bowl and cover with a towel.

Allow dough to rise at room temperature until it doubles in bulk. Then punch down, divide and shape into either 4 small or 2 large loaves. Place into French bread loaf pans that have been greased and sprinkled with cornmeal. If you don't have French bread loaf pans, just place the loaves on a greased and cornmeal-sprinkled cookie sheet. Cover with towels. Allow dough to rise again until double, and then cut several diagonal slashes on top of each loaf. Brush loaves with water. Place on the middle rack of a preheated 375° oven with a shallow pan of water on the bottom rack. Bake 30-45 minutes or until browned. Makes 2 or 4 loaves.

WHOLE WHEAT FRENCH ROLLS

Follow the same procedure as for Whole Wheat French Bread. Instead of shaping it into loaves, though, shape it into either 12 large or 24 smaller rolls. Cut a slash across the top of each one. Bake 15-20 minutes at 375°, or until browned. Makes 12-24 rolls.

PUMPKIN RAISIN MUFFINS

In addition to using canned pumpkin, you can also make these with 2 cups of cooked, fresh pumpkin.

1¾ c. whole wheat flour	⅛ t. each cinnamon, ginger, allspice
1 t. baking powder	1 c. canned pumpkin
½ t. baking soda	1 egg
½ t. salt	½ c. milk
3 T. brown sugar or honey	½ c. raisins (optional)

Preheat oven to 425°. Grease a 12 cup muffin tin well and set aside. In a medium bowl, stir together whole wheat flour, baking powder, baking soda, salt, brown sugar or honey, and spices. In another bowl place the pumpkin, egg and milk. Beat with an electric mixer until well mixed. Pour liquid into flour mixture and stir together until just barely moistened. There may be lumps in the muffin batter. (Overstirring the batter makes the muffins tough.) If desired, stir in raisins. Spoon into muffin tins and place in oven. Bake at 425° for about 20 minutes or until tops are browned. Makes 12 muffins.

OATMEAL HONEY BREAD

This is a somewhat heavy, very satisfying bread. It is especially good with soup.

4 c. warm milk	2 pkg. or 2 T. active dry yeast
½ c. melted butter or margarine	¼ c. warm water
¼ c. honey or brown sugar	10-11 c. whole wheat flour or half
1½ t. salt	whole wheat, half unbleached
2½ c. rolled oats	1 egg, beaten
¾ c. raisins, optional	additional rolled oats

continued on next page

Oatmeal Honey Bread, continued

Combine milk, butter, honey or brown sugar, and salt in a very large bowl. Add oats and raisins. Cover bowl with foil and set aside one hour. At the end of the hour, stir yeast into warm water and let stand until foamy. Then stir yeast into oat mixture. Add flour, stirring continually, until soft dough is formed. Knead for 10 minutes. Place in a greased bowl, cover with a towel, and allow to rise at room temperature until doubled in bulk, about 1½ hours. Punch dough down and shape into three round loaves. Place on greased baking sheets, cover with towels, and allow to rise again until almost doubled. Cut a cross on the top of each loaf, brush with beaten egg, and sprinkle with rolled oats. Bake at 400° for 35 minutes or until loaves are browned and sound hollow when tapped. Makes 3 loaves.

CHEESY BRAN MUFFINS

These are a good, all-purpose muffin and go well with just about any traditional meal.

1 c. whole bran cereal
1¼ c. buttermilk
¼ c. butter or margarine, softened
⅓ c. sugar or honey
1 egg
1½ c. unbleached flour

1½ t. baking powder
½ t. salt
¼ t. baking soda
1 c. shredded cheddar or
    Monterey jack cheese

Place cereal in buttermilk for about 20 minutes to soften. After that, beat butter or margarine and sugar or honey together until fluffy. Add milk and cereal mixture and mix well. In another bowl, stir together the flour, baking powder, salt, baking soda and cheese. Combine the two mixtures, stirring until just moistened. Spoon into greased muffin tins and bake in 400° oven about 20 minutes or until well browned. Makes 12.

BANANA MUFFINS

These muffins are nice for a brunch or tea time. They also go well with a salad luncheon.

1¾ c. unbleached flour
2 t. baking powder
¼ t. baking soda
¾ t. salt
½ t. ground coriander
⅓ c. honey or sugar

1 egg, beaten
1 c. mashed banana
⅓ c. melted butter, margarine or vegetable oil
¼ c. chopped walnuts (optional)

In one bowl, stir together flour, baking powder, baking soda, salt and coriander. In another bowl, combine honey, egg, mashed banana and melted butter or oil. Stir the two mixtures together until barely moistened. If desired, stir in nuts. Spoon into 12 greased muffin cups, filling each two-thirds full. Bake at 400° 15 minutes. Makes 12.

And whatever you do, whether in word or deed, do it all in the name of the Lord Jesus, giving thanks to God the Father through him.

Colossians 3:17

SALADS

Salads add a refreshing touch to all your entertaining. They provide a good balance to heartier main dishes, and they can be the main course at a luncheon or other light meal. Within the salad category itself, the variations are endless. You can make tossed salads, fruit salads, salads with meat, seafood, cheese and eggs.

FROZEN VEGETABLE SALAD

This is one of the all time, most useful salad ideas. You can make it with many variations, and it can be used in a multitude of situations. It is great with any meal, wonderful for a buffet, good to take to a potluck. It can be made up to a day ahead, and doesn't wilt or spoil easily. It's sure to become a favorite in your easy recipe collection.

4 c. frozen vegetables
¼ c. chopped green or regular
   onions, if desired

1 c. Sweet Vinaigrette Dressing
salt and pepper to taste

You can use any kind of frozen vegetable combination you like. Especially useful are the frozen vegetable mixtures such as "Italian vegetables," a wonderful combination of zucchini, cauliflower, carrots, green beans, lima beans and red peppers.

Place the vegetables in a strainer and run warm water over them to thaw slightly. Allow to drain. Place in a medium sized bowl and combine with dressing. Add a few chopped onions if desired. Add salt and pepper to taste and allow to chill 2-3 hours before serving. Serves 4-6.

MARINATED MUSHROOM SALAD

These two mushroom salads are particularly useful for buffets.

5 c. fresh, small mushrooms, or larger ones cut in half
1 16 oz. can tomatoes, diced
½ c. chopped green onion, both the green and white portions

¼ c. vegetable oil
1 t. basil
½ t. dill weed
2 T. fresh parsley, finely chopped
dash salt and pepper

Place oil in a small skillet and saute mushrooms until tender. Then place mushrooms in a medium sized salad bowl with the same oil they were cooked in. Add remaining ingredients and refrigerate. Allow flavors to blend at least a couple of hours before serving. Serves 4.

SWEET POTATO SALAD

A bit different than a regular potato salad, this one has an unusual and sweet taste.

3 medium yams or sweet potatoes
2 T. honey
¼ c. mayonnaise or salad dressing (or more according to the moistness you prefer)

1 apple, cubed
2 stalks celery, diced
¼ c. pecans or walnuts, chopped

Scrub yams, cut in half and boil until tender. When tender, remove from boiling water and let cool slightly. Then peel, cube and place in a medium sized bowl. Heat honey until thin and pour over yams, stirring to coat. Add remaining ingredients, mix gently, and refrigerate until cold. Can be made several hours ahead and refrigerated until serving time. Serves 6.

FRESH MUSHROOM MEDLEY

3 c. sliced, fresh mushrooms   2 T. cider vinegar
1 c. grated carrot   1 t. garlic powder
½ c. celery, finely chopped   1 t. salt
1 2¼ oz. can black olives, chopped   ¼ t. pepper
⅓ c. olive oil

Combine all ingredients in a medium sized bowl and chill several hours before serving. Serves 6.

GREEN BEAN MUSHROOM SALAD

2 c. fresh mushrooms, cleaned and cut into bite-sized pieces
2 c. frozen French cut green beans, thawed
½ c. Mustard French Dressing

Combine above ingredients and chill before serving. Can be made several hours ahead and refrigerated until serving time. Serves 4.

BROCCOLI AND BEAN SALAD

This is a variation of the Frozen Vegetable Salad above. Combine any variety of beans with any frozen vegetable—the combinations are endless. The red and green color combination is particularly nice with this one as part of your holiday entertaining.

4 c. frozen broccoli pieces, thawed
1 15 oz. can red kidney beans, drained
1 cup Sweet Vinaigrette Dressing

Combine all ingredients in a medium sized bowl and let chill before serving. Serves 4-6.

GUACAMOLE SALAD

If you enjoy guacamole dip, you'll love the flavor of this salad.

1 avocado, soft but not overly ripe,
   cut into chunks
juice of one lemon
2 ripe tomatoes, cut into chunks
2 T. red onion, finely minced

½ t. garlic salt
1 2¼ oz. can pitted black olives,
   sliced
¼ c. oil
2 T. chili sauce or salsa

Place avocado pieces in medium sized salad bowl. Add the juice of the lemon and stir, coating avocado pieces well. Add other ingredients and combine. Chill and serve. Serves 4.

PEPPERS IN PEPPERS SLAW

This is a fun salad to serve at a small buffet because you can make each salad in individual green pepper containers and have one for each person.

½ green cabbage, shredded
½ red cabbage, shredded
2 large carrots, shredded
1 red pepper, shredded
1 green pepper, shredded
½ large Spanish onion, chopped
¾ c. honey or sugar

1 c. vegetable oil
1¼ c. white vinegar
½ t. celery seed
¾ t. salt
¾ t. peppers
6 bell peppers, tops cut off and
   cleaned

In a large bowl combine the cabbage, carrots, peppers and onion. On the stove, heat together until boiling the honey or sugar, vegetable oil, vinegar, celery seed, salt and pepper. Pour boiling dressing over cabbage mixture and toss to coat well. Refrigerate overnight or until well chilled. Fill bell peppers with this mixture. Serves 6.

TANGY PASTA SALAD

While many pasta salads are rather bland, the garlic and anchovies in this one will really wake-up your taste buds.

8 oz. pasta (use an interesting shape such as mostacolli)
¼ c. olive oil
2 T. white wine vinegar
1 small jar artichoke hearts in oil
3 garlic cloves, minced quite finely or pressed
1 t. dried oregano
1 t. minced red pepper flakes
1 small can black olives, sliced
¼ c. capers, drained
6 anchovy filets, chopped
½ c. fresh parsley, chopped
15 cherry tomatoes, halved

Cook pasta according to package directions and drain. Cut artichoke hearts into quarters, and then combine the liquid from the jar, the cut hearts, olive oil, wine vinegar, garlic, oregano, and red pepper flakes. Gently combine pasta, anchovies, parsley, tomatoes and olives. Pour the dressing mixture over this and toss gently. Serves 6.

JICAMA PINEAPPLE SLAW

Jicama is a sweet, crisp vegetable that comes from Mexico. You will find it in the produce section of your supermarket.

½ cabbage, chopped or sliced
1 small jicama, peeled and
  shredded
½ c. chopped pecans

1 4 oz. can crushed pineapple,
  drained
½ c. Orange Yogurt Dressing

Combine all ingredients in a medium sized bowl. Chill before serving. Serves 6-8.

ORANGE RICE SALAD

2½ c. water
1 T. chicken bouillon
1 T. butter or margarine
1 c. brown rice
½ c. vegetable oil
½ c. fresh lime juice

2 T. white vinegar
1 T. honey or sugar
1 c. chopped celery
¼ c. chopped green onion
¼ c. chopped pecans
2 small cans mandarin oranges, drained

In a medium sized sauce pan bring water, bouillon and butter to a boil. Pour in rice, lower heat and cook covered until rice is done, about 55 minutes. Remove from heat and allow rice to cool. Mix together vegetable oil, lime juice, white vinegar and honey or sugar. Toss rice with this dressing. Gently stir in celery, green onion, pecans and mandarin oranges. Chill well. Serves 6.

RED CABBAGE SLAW

This is a bit different than the traditional slaws. You'll love the tangy, tart taste and bright color.

1 medium red cabbage, shredded
2 tart apples, grated
¼ c. water
1 t. salt

¼ t. caraway seed
¼ c. cider vinegar
¼ c. honey or brown sugar
¼ c. vegetable oil

Combine shredded cabbage, apples, water, salt and caraway seed in a medium sized ovenproof casserole. Cover and bake at 350° for 45 minutes or until cabbage is tender. Add remaining ingredients and chill before serving. Can be made several hours ahead or the night before and refrigerated until served. Serves 6.

ALMOND SHRIMP SALAD

This salad is super for a ladies luncheon. It also goes well with Chinese Fried Rice.

1 lb. fresh spinach, cleaned and broken into bite-sized pieces	1 2 oz. pkg. almonds, sliced
	1 4 oz. can shrimp pieces
1 10 oz. pkg. frozen, French cut green beans, thawed	½ c. Paprika Dressing

Combine spinach, green beans, almonds and shrimp in a large salad bowl and toss with dressing just before serving. Serves 6.

SOY SHRIMP SALAD

Not only does this salad taste delicious, but the combination of fried rice sticks and spinach creates a very attractive platter. It makes an excellent main dish salad for any luncheon.

The fried rice sticks are clear noodles that turn white and curl up when they are deep fried. They are usually found in the Oriental food section of the grocery store.

2 oz. rice noodles	½ c. sliced radishes
oil for deep-fat frying	½ c. chopped almonds
2 6 oz. cans medium shrimp	10 oz. fresh spinach
1 cucumber, peeled and sliced	Five Spice Dressing

Fry rice noodles in hot oil (365°) a few sticks at a time and drain on paper towels. Tear spinach leaves into bite-sized pieces and line a platter with them. Toss together shrimp, cucumber, radishes and chopped almonds with the Five Spice Dressing. Place rice sticks on top of the spinach and put the shrimp mixture on top of the rice sticks in the center. Serves 4-6.

POMEGRANATE CHRISTMAS SALAD

Generally, pomegranates are in season only around Christmas time. Their bright red color makes the recipe below perfect for holiday meals and buffets.

1 medium sized honeydew melon, peeled and cut into slices
¼ watermelon, seeded and cut into slices
3 kiwi fruit, peeled and cut into slices
2 oranges, seeded and cut into slices
Pomegranate Dressing, full recipe
Reserved pomegranate seeds for garnish

Arrange the fruit on a medium sized platter. Just before serving, pour the dressing over the fruit and garnish with the reserved seeds. Serves 10.

SUGAR-FREE CRANBERRY SALAD

This is quite good, even if made with a sugar-free jello. Though the calorie savings may not seem like much, every little bit helps at holiday time.

1 3 oz. pkg. sugar-free strawberry Jello
1 c. hot water
¾ c. cold water
1 8 oz. can crushed pineapple, in its own juice
1 orange, finely chopped
1 8 oz. can cranberry sauce
2 sticks celery, chopped
¼ c. walnuts, chopped

In a medium sized bowl, place the Jello. Pour boiling water over it and stir until dissolved. Stir in the cold water. Add the crushed pineapple, juice included, and stir. Allow the Jello to chill slightly and then mix in the remaining ingredients. Place the mixture in a serving bowl and allow to chill until set. Serves 6.

SUNNY CITRUS SALAD

This refreshing salad is especially nice served with chicken.

4 bananas, sliced
1 20 oz. can pineapple chunks,
   drained with juice reserved
2 tangerines, cut in pieces

¼ c. flaked coconut
2 T. lime juice
1 T. honey or sugar

Place bananas, pineapple, tangerines and coconut in a medium sized bowl. Combine the reserved pineapple juice, lime juice and honey or sugar in a cup. Stir until the honey or sugar is dissolved in the fruit juices. Moisten the salad with this mixture. (This is not meant to be a "dressing" as such. Its purpose is to just lightly season the fruit.) Serves 4.

MELON PLATTERS

A variety of melons is always a refreshing fruit dish, especially for buffets or brunches. You don't have to do anything except cut them up and arrange them, and they go well with almost any kind of food.

Unless you are having a truly huge buffet or brunch, it is usually wiser to purchase a ready cut half or quarter of several types of melon if you want a variety. If you don't want to serve several kinds, you can limit the platter to only two varieties. Honeydew and watermelon make a nice green and red combination, and honeydew and cantaloupe make a pleasant green and orange arrangement.

The melons can be cut into wedges or slices several hours in advance, put on a platter, covered well and chilled until serving time.

TOSSED SALADS

When we think of salads, the first variety that comes to mind is usually the tossed salad. As tasty as they are, they also pose some problems. Tossed salads tend to wilt after sitting out a while, so we often tend to make them just before the meal is being served and that is when things are most frantic.

To avoid this problem, put your greens and other non-juicy ingredients in the salad bowl and cover with plastic wrap. Put the juicy ingredients, such as tomatoes, in a separate bowl and have your dressing in a cup. It will just take a minute to toss it all together when you are ready to serve.

There are no specific recipes for tossed salads, but you may want to try different types of greens such as various colored leaf lettuce, spinach, romaine or endive lettuce. Tossed salads are a great way to use up odds and ends of fresh vegetables. Most of the dressings in the dressing section work well on tossed salads, so give them a try with your next combination.

SALAD DRESSINGS

Though most of the recipes in this section were created for specific salads in the previous section, they can also be used with any of your own salads. The dressings will keep for at least a week in the refrigerator.

PAPRIKA DRESSING

½ c. honey or sugar
¼ c. salad oil
2 T. lemon juice

1 T. paprika
½ t. dry mustard
1 t. prepared horseradish

Combine all ingredients in a blender or pint jar, making sure the honey or sugar dissolves. Chill well before using. Makes about 1 cup.

FIVE SPICE DRESSING

This dressing has a very distinctive "Oriental" flavor which comes from the sesame oil and the Five Spice Powder. Five Spice Powder is a combination of Oriental spices that can be found in Oriental food stores or the spice department of many supermarkets. The sesame oil is usually found in Oriental food stores. It is an oil used for flavoring, not cooking.

2 T. vegetable oil	1 T. soy sauce
1 T. sesame oil	1 t. honey
2 T. rice vinegar	¼ t. Five Spice Powder

Combine all ingredients in screw top jar and shake until mixed well. Makes about ½ cup.

POMEGRANATE DRESSING

Though this was designed specifically for the Pomegranate Christmas Salad, it is also delicious on any other kind of fruit salad.

1 large, juicy pomegranate	4 oz. cream cheese, softened
1 c. plain yogurt	

Juice the pomegranate. (This is a very messy procedure.) Cut the pomegranate in half and reserve some of the seeds for garnish. Then take each half of the pomegranate and squeeze it with your hand above a strainer placed over a medium sized bowl. You will need ¼ cup juice. When you have the juice, place it with the yogurt and cream cheese in a blender or food processor and puree until smooth. Makes about 1½ cups.

CUCUMBER DRESSING

Cool and refreshing, this dressing is nice for a salad of mixed greens.

1 cucumber, seeded, peeled and then pureed in either a blender or food processor
½ c. sour cream or plain yogurt

½ t. dill weed
¼ t. chervil
¼ c. honey or sugar
dash salt and pepper

Combine all ingredients in a blender or pint jar and chill well before using. Makes about 1¼ cups.

MUSTARD FRENCH DRESSING

This is very tangy and very good on cold vegetable salads.

2 t. honey or sugar
⅓ c. cider vinegar
⅔ c. salad oil
1 t. salt

½ t. pepper
2 T. very grainy, prepared mustard
½ t. garlic powder

Dissolve the honey or sugar in the cider vinegar. Add remaining ingredients and combine in a blender or pint jar. Makes about 1 cup.

ORANGE YOGURT DRESSING

Here is a delicious, easy dressing for any sort of fruit salad, but it is especially good over a citrus salad.

½ c. orange juice   1 c. plain yogurt
2 T. honey or sugar   1 t. grated orange peel

Dissolve the honey or sugar in the orange juice. Then add the remaining ingredients and combine in a blender or pint jar. Makes about 1 cup.

POPPY CURRY DRESSING

The curry flavoring adds an interesting tang to this dressing. Though it is tasty on fruit salads, it is also superb on simple green salads.

¼ c. honey or sugar   ½ c. salad oil
¼ c. cider vinegar   1 t. curry powder

Dissolve the honey or sugar in the cider vinegar. Add the remaining ingredients and combine in a blender or pint jar. Makes about 1 cup.

SWEET SESAME DRESSING

Sweet, but not overly so, this dressing is very nice for fruit salads.

¼ c. honey or sugar
½ c. cider vinegar
½ c. salad oil

2 T. sesame seeds
2 t. poppy seeds
½ t. paprika

Dissolve the honey or sugar in the cider vinegar. Add remaining ingredients and combine in a blender or pint jar. Makes about 1¼ cups.

SOUPS

There are few foods more convenient for the hostess than soup. No last minute preparation, no worries about whether the food will be overcooked or undercooked. Soups can be made months ahead and frozen, or a day ahead and kept in the refrigerator. There are soups for every taste from a cold fruit soup to very hearty stews and chowders. An added plus is that you can make a soup, add some salad and bread, and have a meal to entertain many friends at a very low cost.

SALMON CREAM SOUP

This is very rich and delicious. Serve it on special occasions.

⅓ c. butter or margarine
1 onion, very finely chopped
½ green pepper, very finely chopped
1½ c. mushrooms, sliced
2 T. all-purpose or whole wheat flour
4 c. half and half
2 6 oz. cans salmon
salt and pepper

Melt butter in soup pot. Saute onion, green pepper and mushrooms until onion pieces are clear and other vegetables are tender. Add flour and cook, stirring for 3-4 minutes. Add half and half, stirring constantly, and cook a few minutes until mixture is slightly thick. Add canned salmon. Season to taste with salt and pepper. Heat through and serve. Can be made several hours ahead, refrigerated and then reheated at serving time. Serves 8.

CHILLED FRUIT SOUP

This cold soup can be served either as an appetizer or as a main course for a summer luncheon. If you have never had a fruit soup before, don't be afraid to try it. The taste is delicious.

1 8 oz. pkg. mixed dried fruit, such as the packaged combinations of pitted prunes, peaches, pears and apricots
½ c. raisins
3 c. water
1 apple, cored and chopped
1 lb. mixed frozen fruit, unsweetened
1½ c. dark frozen berries, such as blueberries or boysenberries
½ t. ground coriander
¼ t. ground cinnamon
¼ c. lemon juice
3 T. cornstarch
¾ c. honey or sugar
plain yogurt for garnish

In a medium sized bowl, soak the dried fruit and raisins in the 3 cups of water overnight. The next morning, puree the fruit in the water it was soaked in using a blender or food processor; then place in a large kettle on the stove. Thaw the frozen fruit, puree it with the apple, and add to the dried fruit mixture. Dissolve the cornstarch in the lemon juice and add to the mixture. Add spices and honey or sugar.

Cook gently over medium heat for about 45 minutes, stirring frequently until the soup is slightly thick and the fruit is tender. Be sure it never gets hot enough to scorch. When fruit is tender, chill thoroughly for several hours before serving. It can be made up to 2 days ahead. A spoonful or so of plain yogurt is a tasty garnish when placed on top just before serving. Serves 8.

SPINACH LENTIL SOUP

This soup freezes beautifully so it is easy to make even a month or two in advance if you know you are going to have company. The ingredient combination sounds a bit odd, but it's delicious, and has become a favorite with many of my friends.

2 c. dry lentils	2 stalks celery, finely diced
10 c. water	2 10 oz. pkg. frozen, chopped
½ c. olive oil	spinach
2 T. butter or margarine	¾ c. lemon juice, preferably fresh
1 c. onion, finely diced	salt and pepper to taste
4 cloves garlic, minced or pressed	

Combine lentils and water in a large kettle. Cook lentils until tender. (They can be cooked for about an hour on high heat, and they will be tender, but the soup broth will taste better if the lentils are first brought to a boil and then simmered slowly for 3-4 hours. Cooked this way, the starch from the lentils will naturally thicken and flavor the soup.)

While the lentils are cooking, melt the oil and butter in a medium sized skillet and saute the onion, garlic, and celery over medium heat until the onion pieces are golden. Add this mixture to the cooked lentils. Add spinach, lemon juice, salt and pepper. Cook gently for another 20 minutes to blend flavors. Serves 6-8.

TUNA POTATO SOUP

This is a very hearty soup, great to serve on a winter evening. It is also nice because it is inexpensive and good for those who want to limit their red meat intake.

¼ c. butter or margarine
1 onion, finely chopped
2 stalks celery, finely chopped
8 c. water
3 medium potatoes, cubed
1 4 oz. can tuna

1 16 oz. can tomatoes, chopped, liquid included
1 T. parsley
¼ c. Parmesan cheese
1½ t. salt
½ t. pepper

In large soup pot, melt butter and saute onion and celery until tender (about 5-7 minutes). Add water and cook potatoes 20-30 minutes or until soft. Add tomatoes, tuna, parsley and Parmesan cheese. Season to taste with salt and pepper. Heat through and serve. Can be made a day ahead and reheated at serving time. Serves 8.

MAIN DISHES:
MEAT, POULTRY AND VEGETARIAN ENTREES

TUNA SUPPER PIE

This is similar to a hearty quiche and is a great main dish for a casual supper. The leftovers are also good cold.

1 unbaked pie shell	3 eggs
2 hard-boiled eggs, peeled and sliced	½ c. Monterey jack cheese, grated
1 4 oz. can tuna, drained	1 c. milk
⅓ c. frozen peas, thawed	dash salt and pepper

Place hard-boiled egg slices on the bottom of the uncooked pie crust. Spread tuna over the eggs. Sprinkle peas on top. In a medium bowl combine the eggs, cheese, milk, salt and pepper. Pour this mixture over the tuna. Bake in a 375° oven for about 45 minutes or until lightly browned. Allow to cool a few minutes before slicing. Serves 6-8.

CURRIED SHRIMP AND EGGS

This subtly spiced, creamed dish is delicious for a brunch. It can be made ahead and then reheated just before serving. It is also nice for a light supper when served with a tossed green salad and French bread.

continued on next page

Curried Shrimp and Eggs, continued

3 T. butter or margarine	4 eggs, scrambled
1 t. curry powder	1 4 oz. can shrimp, drained
2 T. flour	4 c. cooked brown rice, wild rice,
2 c. milk	or a combination of both

Melt the butter or margarine in a small saucepan. Add curry powder and flour. Cook 3-4 minutes, stirring constantly. Add milk and continue stirring until thickened. Add eggs and shrimp and stir in gently. Heat through and serve over rice. Serves 4.

CHICKEN AND POULTRY ENTREES

Chicken is a wonderful meat to use as a main dish when entertaining. It is relatively inexpensive, and by adding other ingredients to it, a little bit of chicken can serve many people. Chicken also lends itself to an incredible variety of cooking methods and flavor variations.

The chicken main dishes in this section are very handy for entertaining because they can be assembled early in the day, covered with foil, and placed in the refrigerator. When it is time to bake them, they can be put into the oven and forgotten until they are ready to bring to the table. Or, once the chicken dish is done, you can turn the heat to low if the rest of the meal is not ready or if you want to linger with your guests over appetizers for a bit longer.

For the timid in entertaining, or for anyone desiring an easy and delicious entree, the next five dishes are highly recommended. They are extremely simple to prepare, foolproof in their outcomes, and with a tossed green salad and bread or rolls make a delicious meal. If you have very hearty appetites, serve the chicken dish on some cooked noodles. With a simple dessert, such as ice cream and cookies, you have a meal that is a sure success.

Following the chicken entrees are several for Cornish game hens and for turkey. Both of these poultry items also make the basis for great meals.

LEMON ROSEMARY CHICKEN

This is probably my all time favorite recipe for entertaining. I have literally lost track of how many times it has been served and every time it has been a great favorite. It works well for both small dinner parties and for large, group occasions.

1 chicken, cut-up, with the skin removed	1 t. salt
	2 T. butter or margarine
2 lemons, sliced	¼ c. lemon juice, preferably fresh
1 onion, sliced	½ c. chicken bouillon
1 t. garlic powder	paprika
1 t. rosemary	

Place the chicken in a 9" x 13" baking pan. Arrange the lemon and onion slices on top. Using either a mortar and pestle, a blender, or a food processor, grind together the garlic powder, rosemary and salt. Sprinkle this mixture over the chicken, lemon and onions. Dot the butter or margarine on top. Combine the lemon juice and chicken bouillon and pour over the chicken. Cover with foil and bake in 350° oven for 1½ hours or until done. If desired, just before serving sprinkle on a bit of paprika for additional color. This dish can be assembled up to 8 hours ahead, refrigerated and cooked just before serving. Serves 4.

BAKED MUSTARD CHICKEN

This chicken dish is flavored with a tangy mustard sauce. Be sure to use a good mustard and not the hot dog variety.

1 chicken, cut-up and preferably
  skinned
1 c. frozen cauliflower
1 c. frozen broccoli
½ c. small, fresh mushrooms
1 onion, very thinly sliced

1 T. butter or margarine
2 c. half and half
¼ c. Dijon-style mustard
½ t. dried tarragon
dash salt and pepper

Place the chicken in a 9" x 13" baking pan. Arrange the cauliflower, broccoli, mushrooms and onions on top. Dot on the butter or margarine. In a small bowl, combine the half and half, mustard, tarragon, salt and pepper. Pour this mixture over the chicken and vegetables. Bake in a 350° oven for 1½ hours or until done. Can be assembled up to 8 hours ahead, refrigerated and cooked just before serving. Serves 4.

BROCCOLI CHEESE CHICKEN

1 chicken, cut-up, preferably
  skinned
1 10 oz. pkg. frozen broccoli,
  either spears or large pieces
1 medium onion, thinly sliced
1 T. Worcestershire sauce

1 t. garlic powder
½ t. oregano
dash salt and pepper
2 T. butter or margarine
½ c. Parmesan cheese

Place chicken in 9" x 13" baking pan. Place the broccoli and onion slices on top. Sprinkle with the Worcestershire sauce, garlic powder, oregano, salt and pepper. Dot on pieces of butter or margarine. Top with Parmesan cheese. Cover with foil and bake in 350° oven 1½ hours or until done. Can be assembled up to 8 hours ahead, refrigerated and cooked just before serving. Serves 4.

SOY GARLIC CHICKEN

The Oriental flavor of this dish is good accompanied with brown rice. A fruit salad containing oranges goes with it nicely also.

1 chicken, cut-up and preferably
  skinned
2 t. garlic powder
dash salt and pepper

¼ c. water
½ c. soy sauce
1 bunch green onions, cut into 1
  inch pieces, tops included

Place chicken in a 9" x 13" baking dish. Sprinkle garlic powder, salt and pepper on top. Combine water and soy sauce and pour mixture over chicken. Top with green onions. Cover with foil and bake in a 350° oven for 1½ hours or until done. Can be assembled up to 8 hours ahead, refrigerated and cooked just before serving. Serves 4.

CORNISH GAME HENS

4 Cornish game hens
¼ c. butter or margarine
3 T. honey

2 T. soy sauce
dash salt and pepper
½ c. water

Thaw hens and remove giblets. Place hens in a baking pan. In a small bowl stir together the butter or margarine, honey, soy sauce, salt and pepper. Pat this mixture over the game hens. Pour the water in the bottom of the baking dish. Cover pan with foil and bake for 1 hour at 350°. Remove foil and continue baking until brown for 20-30 minutes. Baste at 10 minute intervals. Serves 4.

CHICKEN WITH TOMATOES

This is good served with pasta and a tossed green salad with Italian dressing.

1 chicken, cut-up and preferably skinned
1½ t. garlic powder
1 t. salt
½ t. pepper
1 T. dried parsley
1 t. oregano
1 t. basil
3 T. butter or margarine
2 medium onions, thinly sliced
1 16 oz. can tomatoes, chopped
2 c. fresh, small, whole mushrooms
1 2¼ oz. can black olives, sliced
⅓ c. lemon juice

Place chicken in a 9" x 13" baking pan. Over the top of the chicken sprinkle the garlic powder, salt, pepper, dried parsley, and oregano. Dot on the butter or margarine. Place the sliced onions, tomatoes, mushrooms and black olives on top. Pour the lemon juice over this. Cover and bake in a 350° oven 1½ hours or until done. Can be assembled up to 8 hours ahead, refrigerated and cooked just before serving. Serves 4.

HERB ROASTED CHICKEN

If you've never baked a chicken whole, you'll be surprised at how yummy it is. The skin on the chicken keeps it moist and flavorful and the spices in the recipe below make it irresistible!

1 3-6 lb. whole chicken
¼ c. honey
½ t. basil
½ t. rosemary
½ t. garlic salt
2 T. butter
½ c. chicken broth

Remove giblets, rinse chicken and pat dry. Place chicken in roasting pan and spread honey over the chicken with a spoon.

continued on next page

Herb Roasted Chicken, continued

Sprinkle the basil, rosemary and garlic salt on top of the chicken. Dot on the butter. Pour chicken broth in the bottom of the pan. Place chicken in a 375° oven and bake approximately 20 minutes per pound. An average 3-4 lb. chicken will take about 1½ hours. Baste every 20-30 minutes. Serves 2-4 depending upon size of chicken.

NOTE: There is no need to buy a roasting chicken which costs more. A fat fryer will do nicely.

LEMON ROASTED GAME HENS

¼ c. lemon juice
½ c. olive oil
¼ c. white vinegar
¼ t. tabasco sauce
1 t. salt
1 T. honey or sugar

¼ t. garlic powder
1 t. paprika
1 fresh lemon thinly sliced
1 small onion thinly sliced
2 game hens, either whole or
    split

Combine all ingredients except game hens. Marinate hens overnight in the mixture. If the hens are whole, marinate them in a bowl, turning several times. Bake at 350° 40-60 minutes, basting frequently with the marinade. The hens are delicious hot or cold.

NOTE: To split game hens: Allow the hens to thaw and then cut in half with a strong pair of kitchen shears or a sharp knife. The split halves can also be cut into quarters if desired. Serves 2-4.

ORANGE GLAZED CORNISH GAME HENS

2 Cornish game hens   1 t. orange peel
2 T. butter or margarine, softened   ½ c. orange juice

Thaw game hens and remove giblets. Rinse and pat dry. Place hens in baking dish. Stir orange peel into softened butter or margarine. Pat butter mixture on the hens. Pour orange juice over them. Bake in 375° oven 45-60 minutes, basting every 15 minutes. Serves 2.

TURKEY GRAVY

2 T. cornstarch   5 c. drippings from the cooked
½ c. whole milk   turkey
2½ c. whole milk   salt and pepper to taste

Dissolve the cornstarch in ½ cup milk. Add this mixture and the additional 2½ cups milk to the drippings and cook, stirring constantly, until the mixture thickens. Season to taste with salt and pepper. Makes 8 cups.

SWEET BARBECUE SAUCE

⅓ c. cider vinegar   1 t. chili powder
½ c. honey or brown sugar   ½ t. garlic powder
1 c. catsup   ½ t. paprika
½ c. water   2 T. Worcestershire sauce
1 t. dry mustard   salt and pepper to taste

Dissolve honey or brown sugar in vinegar. Place remaining ingredients in a blender or food processor and add vinegar mixture. Blend until well mixed. Makes about 2½ cups.

BARBECUED TURKEY HINDQUARTER

Turkey hindquarters are a great way to eat turkey any time of the year. They are low in cost and without the fuss of a huge turkey. They can be baked or treated to a yummy sauce as in the recipe below.

1 turkey hindquarter, 3-4 lb. in weight
1 c. barbecue sauce, either prepared or made with the recipe below

Thaw turkey hindquarter in the refrigerator. Remove from packaging, and set giblets aside. Rinse hindquarter and pat dry. Place in baking pan and bake covered with foil at 350° for 1 hour. At the end of that time, baste hindquarter with barbecue sauce and bake for an additional 2-3 hours turning the hindquarter and basting it every 30 minutes until meat is done and registers 185° on a meat thermometer inserted into the thickest part of the meat. If you don't have a meat thermometer, prick the meat near the thigh joint. If the juice runs clear, the meat is done. Serves 4.

BEST EVER TURKEY

Turkey is a great dish for entertaining anytime. The one problem many people have with turkey, however, is that it comes out of the oven too dry. The method below overcomes that problem and works well with even inexpensive turkeys because the turkey is steamed as it bakes in the various flavorful ingredients. For this method to be successful, you will need a roasting pan with a lid.

1 turkey, 12-20 lb.
½ c. butter or margarine
½ t. salt
¼ t. pepper

1 t. garlic powder
2 t. poultry seasoning
1 c. chicken broth

continued on next page

Best Ever Turkey, continued

Place the turkey in a roasting pan. Pat the butter or margarine over it. Sprinkle some of the spices on top of the turkey and some of them inside the cavity. Pour the chicken broth inside the cavity of the turkey. Put the lid on the roasting pan and bake the turkey in a 325° oven. The cooking time will vary depending upon the weight. Plan on about 20 minutes per pound. Or, if you are using a meat thermometer, allow the temperature to reach 190°. Baste every ½ hour or so during the baking process. During the last hour, remove the lid if the turkey needs to brown more. The number of servings will depend upon the weight of the turkey.

For food safety and ease in preparation, bake the dressing separately. See the section on Vegetables and Side Dishes for recipes.

OVEN BARLEY BEEF

Here is a hearty winter stew you can simply assemble, put in the oven and forget about until serving time. It is great for an after sledding or ice skating party. It can also be put in the oven while you attend evening church, and then served to friends invited over for an after church supper.

1½ lb. beef stew meat	1 t. honey
½ c. barley	2 t. Worcestershire sauce
3 T. minced onion	2 t. garlic salt
2 bay leaves	2 c. small, fresh mushrooms
3 whole allspice	4 c. water
2 T. soy sauce	dash pepper

Combine all ingredients in a 2½ quart baking dish. Bake in 350° oven for 3 hours or until meat is tender and barley cooked. Can be made a day ahead and reheated. Serves 6-8.

OVEN GREEN CHILI

This is easy to make and very versatile. The chili can be served in bowls with flour tortillas alongside, or it can be used to make the enchiladas below. The Green Chili can also be served over eggs or used to top any Mexican dish you desire. It and the enchiladas can be made up to a day ahead, refrigerated and reheated at serving time.

1½ lb. beef stew meat or round
   steak, cut into small chunks
2 onions, diced
1 2½ oz. can green chilis, chopped
3 cloves garlic, minced or pressed

1 t. ground cumin
½ t. chili powder (or more to taste)
1 32 oz. can tomatoes, chopped
¼ c. water

Combine all ingredients in a 2½ quart baking dish. Cook 3 hours at 350° or until meat is tender. Serves 4.

NOTE: Green chilis are fairly mild. For a hot green chili, you may want to throw in a few jalapenos or any other favorite chili pepper.

GREEN CHILI ENCHILADAS

Oven Green Chili, recipe above
6 flour tortillas

Cook chili as above. When finished, put about 2 tablespoons chili inside each flour tortilla. Roll up and place in a 9" x 13" baking dish. Pour remaining chili over all. Heat through in either oven or microwave and serve hot. Serves 4.

GREEN CHILI ENCHILADAS WITH CHEESE

Oven Green Chili, recipe above   ½ lb. cheddar cheese, grated
6 flour tortillas

Divide cheese into 6 portions. Put each portion in a flour tortilla, roll and place in a 9" x 13" baking pan. Pour green chili over all. Cover and heat in a 350° oven for 30 minutes or until heated through. Serves 4.

SPAGHETTI ALA CARBONARA

This traditional Italian dish originated long ago in the forests of Abruzzi. The *carbonara* were charcoal makers who would camp in the woods for days tending their fires to make charcoal. They would bring spaghetti, olive oil, cheese and eggs along with their smoked hams to make this hearty and delicious main dish. The preparation of this dish is similar to making fettucini.

1 lb. spaghetti or fettucini noodles
6 slices bacon, cut into little pieces
2 T. olive oil
2 T. butter
¼ c. ham, cut into small slices (Proscuitto is best, but regular ham can be
    used if proscuitto is not available.)
3 eggs
⅔ c. grated Parmesan and Romano cheese mixture
lots of freshly ground black pepper

While spaghetti is cooking, fry the bacon. When it is almost done, drain off grease. Add the olive oil and butter and melt. Add the ham and cook while beating together the eggs and the cheese. As soon as the spaghetti is done, drain quickly and turn onto a hot platter. Pour egg and cheese mixture into hot ham and bacon mixture and cook 1 minute. Toss quickly into the pasta and serve. The hot pasta will finish cooking the eggs. Serves 4-6.

VEGETARIAN ENTREES

The gracious hostess always has a number of vegetarian recipes in her repertoire for the increasing number of individuals who prefer this way of eating. And, vegetarian main dishes are not just for vegetarians. They are a wonderfully tasty change for meat eaters as well. All of the dishes in the following section are healthy and satisfying no matter how hearty the appetite you wish to please. Try at least one vegetarian main dish at your next buffet. You'll be surprised at the number of people who will enjoy it.

SPINACH LASAGNA

Lasagna is a perennial favorite. Try this yummy version using a cheese and spinach mixture instead of hamburger.

Lasagna Sauce:
1 medium onion, chopped	1 t. basil
2 cloves garlic, minced or pressed	½ t. ground oregano
¼ c. olive oil	2 t. fresh parsley, chopped
1 16 oz. can tomato sauce	

Saute the onion and garlic in olive oil over medium heat until tender. Add remaining ingredients and simmer about 10 minutes.

Lasagna Assembly:
1 10 oz. pkg. frozen chopped spinach, thawed and drained	1 t. pepper
1 c. cottage or ricotta cheese	8 oz. lasagna noodles, cooked according to package directions
2 T. Parmesan cheese	1 c. grated mozzarella cheese
1 egg	sauce recipe above
1 t. salt	

continued on next page

163

Spinach Lasagna, continued

Combine the spinach, cottage or ricotta cheese, Parmesan cheese, egg, salt and pepper. In a 9" x 9" baking dish, place a layer of lasagna noodles and then layer the ingredients in this order: spinach/cheese mixture, lasagna noodles, grated mozzarella cheese, lasagna sauce. Repeat, layering at least twice. Top with a sprinkling of Parmesan cheese. Bake uncovered in a 350° oven 30-40 minutes or until heated through and bubbly. Serves 4-6. Can be assembled up to 8 hours ahead and baked just before serving.

This recipe can be doubled and baked in a 9" x 13" pan. Increase baking time about 10 minutes.

MANICOTTI CHEESE SAUCE

⅓ c. butter or margarine
3 T. flour
1½ c. milk

¼ c. Parmesan cheese
1 T. fresh parsley, finely chopped
dash salt and pepper

Melt butter in a medium sized saucepan. Add flour and stir for several minutes until flour is cooked. Add milk, stirring constantly until thickened. Stir in Parmesan cheese, parsley and dash of salt and pepper. Pour cheese over stuffed manicotti shells and bake as directed above.

SPINACH MANICOTTI

Though the filling is similar to the Spinach Lasagna recipe, the Manicotti has a flavor all of its own because it is topped with a cheese, instead of a tomato based sauce.

1 egg
1 lb. ricotta cheese
1 10 oz. pkg. frozen chopped
   spinach, thawed and drained
½ c. grated Parmesan cheese
2 T. fresh parsley, finely chopped
½ t. salt

¼ t. pepper
1 16 oz. pkg. manicotti shells,
   cooked according to package
   directions
Manicotti Cheese Sauce, recipe
   below

NOTE: To make manicotti shells easier to stuff, boil them until tender, then place cooking pot in the sink and gradually pour in cold water while draining off hot water. Allow shells to soak in cool water until ready to stuff. Shells will retain their shape in the cool water until you are ready to use them.

Combine egg, ricotta cheese, drained spinach, Parmesan cheese, parsley, salt and pepper. Carefully stuff cooked manicotti shells with spinach mixture and place in a greased 9" x 13" baking dish. When all shells have been filled, set aside and make the Manicotti Cheese Sauce. Pour cheese sauce over stuffed shells and bake uncovered at 375° for 20 minutes, or until sauce is bubbly. Makes 4-6 servings.

We always thank God, the Father of our Lord Jesus Christ, when we pray for you, because we have heard of your faith in Christ Jesus and of the love you have for all the saints.

Colossians 1:3-4

VEGETABLES AND SIDE DISHES

Vegetables and side dishes round out a menu. For flavor, color, vitamins, and fiber, you can't beat vegetables for their yummy taste and healthful addition to your entertainment menus.

ORANGE WILD RICE STUFFING

½ c. wild rice
1 c. water
3 c. bread cubes
1 11 oz. can mandarin oranges,
  drained (reserve liquid)
½ c. celery, chopped
⅓ c. onion, chopped
⅓ c. melted butter or margarine

⅓ c. chicken broth
reserved liquid from mandarin
  oranges
1 t. orange peel
½ t. lemon peel
½ t. salt
1 t. curry powder

Bring 1 cup water to boil in saucepan. Add ½ cup wild rice. Place lid on pan and turn heat to low. Cook until rice is done, about 30-45 minutes.

In a large bowl toss together the cooked wild rice, bread cubes, mandarin oranges, celery and onion. In another bowl, combine the melted butter or margarine, chicken broth, reserved liquid from the mandarin oranges, orange peel, lemon peel, salt and curry powder. Pour this mixture over the bread crumb mixture and toss gently to combine. Place mixture in a buttered baking dish and bake, covered, for the last hour of the poultry's cooking. For a crispy stuffing, remove foil the last half hour. Serves 4.

167

MAPLE WHIPPED SWEET POTATOES

These simply melt in your mouth.

1 32 oz. can sweet potatoes
¼ c. maple syrup
2 T. butter or margarine, softened

additional cream or milk
butter and cinnamon for garnish

Cook sweet potatoes in the juice they come in until heated through. Remove from heat. Beat with an electric mixer until broken up. Add maple syrup and butter or margarine. Continue beating until fluffy, adding additional milk or cream if needed. Spoon into serving bowl and garnish with a spoonful of butter or margarine and a sprinkle of cinnamon. Serves 4.

NOTE: The recipe above can also be made with any cooked, fresh squash such as acorn, butternut or turban. It can also be made with fresh cooked yams or pumpkin.

APPLE SAUSAGE STUFFING

½ lb. sausage, fried and crumbled
6 c. bread cubes
1 apple, chopped
½ c. celery, chopped
⅓ c. onions, chopped

⅓ c. raisins
⅓ c. melted butter or margarine
1 c. chicken broth
¼ t. garlic salt

In a large bowl, toss together the sausage, bread cubes, apple, celery, onions and raisins. In another bowl combine the melted butter or margarine, chicken broth and garlic salt. Pour this over the bread cube mixture and toss gently to combine. Place in buttered pan and bake, covered, for the last hour of the poultry's baking. To make the stuffing crunchy, remove foil for the last half hour. Serves 4-6.

STEAMED BROCCOLI WITH BASIL BUTTER

It doesn't take much work to take an ordinary vegetable and make it special as this simple and delicious recipe illustrates.

1 lb. fresh or frozen broccoli, cut into bite-sized pieces
⅓ c. butter, melted
½ t. basil

Steam fresh or frozen broccoli until barely tender, retaining the bright green color. In a small pan, melt the butter and stir in the basil. Cook over very low heat about 5 minutes. This allows the flavor of the basil to permeate the butter. Just before serving, toss the broccoli gently with the basil butter. Serves 4.

NOTE: This same recipe can be used in a variety of ways by simply substituting green beans, peas, brussel sprouts or small artichokes for the broccoli.

NUTTY STUFFING

6 c. dry bread cubes
½-1 c. cooked, cut-up giblets
½ c. almonds, chopped
½ c. raw sunflower seeds
1 c. celery, chopped
⅔ c. onion, chopped
⅓ c. melted butter or margarine
1 c. chicken broth
2 T. Spike or any seasoning salt

In a large bowl toss together the bread cubes, giblets, almonds, sunflower seeds, celery and onion. In a small bowl combine the melted butter or margarine, chicken broth and the Spike or seasoning salt. Pour over the bread cube mixture and toss to combine well. Place in a buttered baking dish and bake, covered with foil, for the last hour the poultry is cooking. If you want your stuffing to be crunchy, remove the foil for the last half hour. Serves 4-6.

POPPY SEED NOODLES

This mild noodle side dish is good to serve with any casserole or dish with a flavorful sauce. Any of the chicken dishes work well in this way.

1 8 oz. pkg. egg ribbon noodles, cooked according to package directions and then drained and rinsed
¼ c. melted butter or margarine
1 t. poppy seeds
dash salt and pepper

Toss cooked noodles with butter or margarine, poppy seeds, salt and pepper in a large bowl. Transfer to a medium sized casserole. Either serve immediately, or make several hours ahead, refrigerate covered and then reheat in oven or microwave just before serving. Serves 6.

ORANGE FLAVORED CARROTS

4 c. sliced carrots
½ c. orange juice

2 T. honey or brown sugar
½ t. ground coriander

Combine all ingredients in a medium sized bowl. then place carrots in a casserole and bake uncovered for 35 minutes at 400° or until carrots are tender. Serves 6.

SPANISH MACARONI

This is a perfect side dish for any sort of Mexican meal.

5 c. cooked pasta, preferably
  elbow macaroni
1 16 oz. can tomatoes, chopped
1 4 oz. can mushrooms

¼ c. cheddar cheese, grated
¼ c. salsa
¼ c. cheddar cheese, grated

Combine all ingredients except for ¼ cup of the grated Cheddar cheese in a medium sized casserole dish. Sprinkle remaining cheese on top and heat in a 350° oven until cheese melts, about 15-20 minutes. Serves 4-6.

Dear friend, you are faithful in what you are doing for the brothers, even though they are strangers to you . . . . We ought therefore to show hospitality to such men so that we may work together for the truth.

III John 5-8

DESSERTS

Desserts are always a delight whether as the ending to a wonderful meal or the sweet balance during a party filled with tangy and salty foods. Desserts do not have to be complex to be well received. None of the recipes below are, but each is delicious.

SUGARLESS FRUIT PIE

This is a good recipe to have in your cooking file because, in addition to being quite tasty, it is perfect for guests who cannot have sugar. The sweetness in the pie comes from the fruit sugar in the apple juice concentrate and from the fruit itself.

2 T. cornstarch
enough water to dissolve
   cornstarch
1 12 oz. can frozen apple juice
   concentrate
4 c. fresh or frozen fruit (peaches, apricots, cherries, and apples all work nicely) NOTE: If you use frozen fruit, be sure it is the kind that is frozen without added sugar.

¼ t. almond extract
1 T. vanilla extract
2 t. ground coriander
1 unbaked pie shell

Dissolve cornstarch in water. Combine with other ingredients in a medium sized saucepan. Bring mixture to a boil, then lower heat and cook, stirring frequently until thick. Pour into unbaked pie shell and bake at 375° for 30 minutes or until crust is brown and fruit tender. Serve 6-8.

LEMON SAUCE

This sauce is not only good on the Applesauce Bundt Cake, above, but it is also delicious on any sort of spicy cake or bread pudding.

1 c. water
1 T. cornstarch
1 c. honey
½ c. lemon juice

3 T. butter or margarine
2 T. lemon rind or ½ t. lemon extract

In a medium sized saucepan, combine water and cornstarch. Put on low heat and add honey and lemon juice. Cook, stirring constantly, until thick. Turn off heat and stir in butter and lemon rind or extract. Good hot or cold. Makes about 2½ cups.

APPLESAUCE BUNDT CAKE

Bundt cakes are great for entertaining. You don't have to worry about them falling. The shape of the pan almost guarantees that they will come out great. They look nice on a buffet table; serve lots of people, and are so tasty.

2¼ c. whole wheat pastry flour or unbleached flour
½ t. salt
2 t. baking soda
1 t. ground cinnamon
1 t. ground nutmeg
1 t. ground coriander
½ c. raisins

½ c. chopped walnuts
⅓ c. butter or margarine, melted
1 c. honey or brown sugar
1 egg
¼ c. plain yogurt
1 c. applesauce
Lemon Sauce, recipe below

continued on next page

Applesauce Bundt Cake, continued

Thoroughly grease and flour a 9" bundt cake pan. Stir together flours, salt, soda, spices, raisins and walnuts. In another bowl, blend together butter, honey, egg, yogurt and applesauce. Combine the dry ingredients with the moist ingredients and pour into bundt pan. Bake in 350° oven 30 minutes, or until a toothpick inserted in center of cake comes out clean. Invert cake pan and allow cake to cool on wire rack. Excellent topped with Lemon Sauce or whipped cream. Serves 12.

LEMON SNOWBALLS

When in doubt about what to serve for dessert, a plate of cookies is always nice.

⅔ c. honey or sugar
½ c. butter or margarine, softened
2 t. grated lemon rind
1 egg
3 T. lemon juice
2½ c. unbleached flour

¼ t. baking soda
½ t. salt
¼ t. cream of tartar
¼ c. flaked coconut
¼ c. almonds, finely chopped

Cream together honey or sugar and butter or margarine in a medium sized bowl. Add grated lemon rind, egg, lemon juice, and cream well. In a separate bowl mix the flour, baking soda, salt, and cream of tartar. Add this to liquid mixture and combine well. Stir in coconut and almonds. Form dough into walnut-sized balls and place on an ungreased cookie sheet, or simply drop dough by teaspoonfuls on to cookie sheet. Bake in preheated 350° oven for 10-15 minutes or until very lightly browned. If desired, the cookies may be frosted with Cookie Frosting and additional coconut or almonds sprinkled on top. Makes about 4 dozen.

CRUNCHY PEANUT BUTTER COOKIES

1 c. crunchy peanut butter
1 c. sugar or ¾ c. honey
1 egg

1 t. vanilla
1 c. flour
¼ c. chopped peanuts

Beat together the peanut butter and the sugar or honey. Add the egg and vanilla and beat again. Stir in flour, and then add the peanuts. Drop by teaspoonfuls onto an ungreased baking sheet. Make a cross pattern with a fork on each cookie. Bake in a preheated 325° oven 15-18 minutes or until very lightly browned. Makes 16-24.

CAROB CASHEW COOKIES

The carob gives a chocolate flavor to these healthy cookies.

½ c. butter or margarine, softened
½ c. honey or sugar
2 eggs
1 t. vanilla extract
½ t. baking powder
½ t. salt

1 c. whole wheat pastry flour or unbleached flour
¾ c. carob flour
½ c. pecans, chopped
½ c. raw and unsalted cashews, chopped

Cream together butter or margarine and sugar or honey in a large mixing bowl. Beat in the eggs and vanilla. In a medium sized bowl, combine the baking powder, salt, flour and carob. Stir the flour mixture into the butter mixture. Add pecans and cashews and mix. Drop dough by teaspoonfuls onto a greased cookie sheet and flatten with the tines of a fork. Bake at 325° for 10-15 minutes or until set. Makes about 3 dozen cookies.

COOKIE FROSTING

This easy-to-make frosting is wonderful on all kinds of cookies. You can vary the flavoring to suit your taste by replacing all or part of the vanilla flavoring called for with lemon, almond, orange or any other flavoring you might enjoy.

4 oz. cream cheese, softened   1 t. vanilla
2 T. butter, softened   2 T. honey or sugar

Cream all ingredients together well. This makes enough frosting for about 2-3 dozen cookies if spread lightly.

HAZELNUT BROWNIES

4 oz. unsweetened chocolate   1 t. vanilla
½ c. butter or margarine   1 c. flour
1½ c. sugar or 1¼ c. honey   ¼ t. salt
3 eggs   ⅔ c. chopped hazelnuts or filberts

Melt chocolate. Cream together the butter or margarine and honey or sugar. Add eggs one at a time and beat well after each addition. Mix in vanilla and melted chocolate. Combine flour and salt, then add to mixture. Add nuts. Spoon batter into a greased 9" square baking pan. Bake in preheated 375° oven about 30 minutes. Cool and cut into squares. Makes about 16-24 squares.

SPECIAL ICE CREAM TREATS

Sometimes some of the most healthful and delicious desserts are also the most obvious and easy to prepare. Ice cream fits into this category. Today there are a multitude of delicious natural ice creams available made with honey and no unnatural additives. There are even frozen treats made with tofu and other non-dairy items that are perfect for individuals who are allergic to milk products.

Most of these are quite good by themselves and great to keep on hand for any sort of entertaining. If you have some in the freezer, you are never without a quick dessert for any meal.

To dress up your frozen treat, sprinkle granola, nuts or a prepared topping over it. Maple syrup is also delicious as are any of the fruit syrups. If you want to make it extra special, try some of the recipes below.

FRUIT AND HONEY TOPPING

2 T. cornstarch
¼ c. water
1 c. apple juice
¼ c. honey

1 c. frozen fruit: strawberries, blueberries or peaches work the best

Dissolve the cornstarch in ¼ cup water and place in a medium sized saucepan. Add juice and honey. Stir over medium heat until the mixture thickens, bubbles and finally clears. Add fruit and cook a few more minutes. Remove from heat and serve. Makes about 2¼ cups.

TOASTED PECANS

You won't believe how fantastic these taste over a good vanilla ice cream. They are easy to prepare, but what a special treat!

¼ c. butter   1 c. pecans

Melt butter in a medium sized saucepan. Add finely chopped pecans. Keep mixture over medium heat for about 10 minutes, stirring constantly. If the nuts begin to stick, add a bit more butter. Serve immediately over ice cream. Makes 1 cup.

SPICED HONEY NUT SAUCE

1 c. honey
1 t. ground cinnamon
1 t. orange peel
⅛ t. mace
½ c. milk

2 t. butter or margarine
1 t. vanilla extract
2 c. chopped nuts, unsalted and unroasted, such as a combination of walnuts, cashews or almonds

Combine honey, seasonings and milk in a medium sized saucepan. Cook for about 5 minutes over medium heat, stirring constantly. Remove from heat and stir in the butter. Allow to melt 1-2 minutes, then add the vanilla and nuts. The sauce can be served right away or stored in the refrigerator and used later. Makes about 3½ cups.

VELVET PUMPKIN CHEESECAKE

This is so tasty it almost shouldn't be eaten. Not only is it an excellent substitute for traditional holiday pumpkin pie, but it is a delicious and appropriate dessert for any time of the year.

2 T. butter or margarine, softened	2 T. flour
⅓ c. graham cracker crumbs	½ t. cinnamon
¼ t. cinnamon	¼ t. ginger
¼ t. ginger	½ t. allspice
1 lb. cream cheese, softened	⅛ t. salt
½ c. brown sugar	8 oz. cream cheese
½ c. maple syrup	½ t. vanilla
4 eggs	2 T. sugar or honey
1 c. pumpkin	

Butter well a 10″ spring form pan with the 2 tablespoons of softened butter or margarine. In a small bowl, stir together the graham cracker crumbs, cinnamon and ginger. Sprinkle this mixture around the bottom and sides of the spring form pan. Evenly distribute any excess crumb mixture on the bottom of the pan.

In a large mixing bowl, beat 1 lb. of the cream cheese until fluffy. Add the brown sugar and beat to combine well. Add the maple syrup and beat again. Add the eggs one by one and beat thoroughly after each addition. Add the pumpkin and beat in well.

In a small bowl, stir together the spices, salt and flour. Beat into mixture. Spoon mixture into spring form pan and bake in a 325° oven for 1 hour or until very lightly browned. Remove cheesecake from oven and allow to cool 10 minutes. While cheesecake is cooling, beat together 8 oz. cream cheese, vanilla and sugar/honey. Spoon this mixture over the cheesecake and return to oven. Bake an additional 10 minutes. Chill cheesecake well, at least 5 hours, before serving. Serves 12.

CHERRY MINCEMEAT PIE

The red cherries combined with the mincemeat lighten the taste while adding a hearty plus to cherry pie. Serve it for the holidays or any time of year.

1 16 oz. can tart red cherries,
  drained
2 c. prepared mincemeat

1 unbaked pie shell
sweetened whipped cream

Combine cherries and mincemeat. Spoon into an unbaked pie shell. Bake at 350° about 30 minutes or until crust is browned. Remove from oven and cool. Just before serving, garnish with whipped cream. Serves 6.

We ought always to thank God for you, brothers, and rightly so, because your faith is growing more and more, and the love every one of you has for each other is increasing.

II Thessalonians 1:3

INDEX

Desserts   173

ALPHABETICAL INDEX OF RECIPES

A

B

C

E

F

G

H

J

L

M

N

O

P

R

S

T

V

W

Above all, love each other deeply, because love covers over a multitude of sins. Offer hospitality to one another without grumbling.

I Peter 4:8-9